Eudaimonia

Eudaimonia: Perspectives for Music Learning asserts the fertile applications of eudaimonia—an Aristotelian concept of human flourishing intended to explain the nature of a life well lived—for work in music learning and teaching in the twenty-first century. Drawing insights from within and beyond the field of music education, contributors reflect on what the "good life" means in music, highlighting issues at the core of the human experience and the heart of schooling and other educational settings. This pursuit of personal fulfillment through active engagement is considered in relation to music education as well as broader social, political, spiritual, psychological, and environmental contexts. Especially pertinent in today's complicated and contradictory world, *Eudaimonia: Perspectives for Music Learning* is a concise compendium on this oft-overlooked concept, providing musicians with an understanding of an ethically guided and socially meaningful music-learning paradigm.

Gareth Dylan Smith is Assistant Professor of Music (Music Education) at Boston University, a founding editor of the *Journal of Popular Music Education,* and a drummer.

Marissa Silverman is Associate Professor of Music at the John J. Cali School of Music at Montclair State University.

Routledge New Directions in Music Education Series

Series Editor: Clint Randles

The **Routledge New Directions in Music Education Series** consists of concise monographs that attempt to bring more of the wide world of music, education, and society into the discourse in music education.

Eco-Literate Music Pedagogy
Daniel J. Shevock

The Music Profiles Learning Project
Let's Take This Outside
Radio Cremata, Joseph Michael Pignato, Bryan Powell, and Gareth Dylan Smith

A Different Paradigm in Music Education
Re-examining the Profession
David A. Williams

Eudaimonia
Perspectives for Music Learning
Edited by Gareth Dylan Smith and Marissa Silverman

Eudaimonia

Perspectives for Music Learning

Edited by Gareth Dylan Smith and Marissa Silverman

NEW YORK AND LONDON

First published 2020
by Routledge
52 Vanderbilt Avenue, New York, NY 10017

and by Routledge
2 Park Square, Milton Park, Abingdon, Oxon, OX14 4RN

Routledge is an imprint of the Taylor & Francis Group, an informa business

Library of Congress Cataloging-in-Publication Data
A catalog record for this title has been requested

ISBN: 978-0-367-21029-8 (hbk)
ISBN: 978-0-367-49813-9 (pbk)
ISBN: 978-0-429-26494-8 (ebk)

Typeset in Times New Roman
by Wearset Ltd, Boldon, Tyne and Wear

Contents

Series Foreword

The Routledge New Directions in Music Education Series consists of concise monographs that attempt to bring more of the wide world of music, education, and society—and all of the conceptualizations and pragmatic implications that come with that world—into the discourse of music education. It is about discovering and uncovering big ideas for the profession, criticizing our long-held assumptions, suggesting new courses of action, and putting ideas into motion for the prosperity of future generations of music makers, teachers of music, researchers, scholars, and society.

Clint Randles, Series Editor

Preface

The thinking and activist apparatus of eudaimonia has become so important for both of us over the last several years, thus the impulse to curate this collection. The concept of "eudaimonia" provides especially fertile ground for work in music and learning. However, resources that discuss eudaimonia, music, and learning in one place are relatively scarce. Therefore, we felt there ought to be *somewhere* that collated writings on these topics, at the very least to provide a jumping-off point for further exploration. Music learning never takes place in a vacuum. Musicians of all stripes and stages constantly draw inspiration and provocation from action and thought in spaces and places that are not explicitly musical or pedagogical. Music-making beings undertake their work and make sense of their lives and relationships in the full richness of the joys, challenges, ambiguities, and contradictions of the world. For this reason, this volume houses some contributors who deal directly with music and learning while others write about the broader social, political, ethical, spiritual, psychological, environmental, and philosophical contexts in which people act out their lives. The thread of eudaimonia unites these essays; all speak to aspects of how to live well and flourish—ideals which for many people music must involve making music.

Both editors work in the field of music education and both have arrived here through specializing in adjunct fields; although we have earned eight degrees between us, only one of these is in music education. Much of what we bring to the field comes from music and music-learning contexts outside of educational establishments, which is why we made an eleventh-hour decision to change the title of this book from *Eudaimonia: Perspectives for Music Education*, to *Eudaimonia: Perspectives for Music Learning*. This small semantic shift is important, as we believe the writing in here 1) examines much more than what may be bounded by the phrase "music education," and 2) speaks to colleagues interested in music doing and music learning, broadly construed. Notably, we were keen to include voices of scholars who speak about eudaimonia without necessarily relating it much or indeed at all to music learning, and whose work can deeply inform debate and discussion, enriching mindful praxis of readers—ourselves included. We relish the opportunity to live with the questions, comforts, and challenges of eudaimonia: perspectives for music learning.

We are very grateful that the esteemed authors whose work is included herein agreed to be part of this collection—thank you. We wish to acknowledge the help of Yunshu Tan, who assisted with the consistency of formatting references for this book; thank you, Yunshu. We would also like to thank the New Directions series editor, Clint Randles, and Constance Ditzel at Routledge for seeing value in our vision for the volume and for supporting it all the way to publication. The theme of *Eudaimonia: Perspectives for Music Learning* seems especially well-suited to this book series that aims at "putting ideas into motion for the prosperity of future generations of music makers, teachers of music, and society" (Randles, 2019).

Gareth Dylan Smith and Marissa Silverman
January 1, 2020

Reference

Randles, C. (2019). Routledge new directions in music education series. Retrieved from: http://clintrandles.com/?page_id=89. [Accessed 7.12.2019].

1 Eudaimonia

Flourishing through Music Learning

Gareth Dylan Smith and Marissa Silverman

What is "Eudaimonia"?

In *After virtue*, philosopher Alasdair MacIntyre (2007) draws our attention to a potential, fictional world in which our planet experiences "catastrophic" environmental disasters, the cause of which are blamed on all scientists. The result of such catastrophe is not only "riots," but also the "laboratories are burnt down, physicists are lynched, books and instruments are destroyed" (p. 1). Furthermore, in MacIntyre's "imaginary" world, "a Know-Nothing political movement takes power" and removes science from the curriculum in schools and universities, and imprisons and executes any scientists left in the world (p. 1). MacIntyre continues to imagine further results of this, including but not limited to an eventual reimagining of science based on half-truths which, in turn, would promote pseudoscience and a language that is as imprecise as it is harmful. This is not a wholly original premise. Dystopian writers have created similar-sounding spaces (e.g., *Brave new world, 1984, The handmaid's tale*).

Still, MacIntyre's thought experiment reveals how easy it is to lose "our comprehension, both theoretical and practical," and, most importantly perhaps, our morality (p. 2). And what might the more pernicious result of this be? According to MacIntyre, in the end, unless we rightly understand the world in which we live, and make value judgements that are ethically and truthfully sound, we cannot have any hope of living humanistically or purposefully, or, in others words, virtuously. Where do we learn how to live virtuously? According to MacIntyre—who interprets and expands upon Aristotle and Thomas Aquinas—"it is always through the engagement" in "a variety of practices, including those of making and sustaining families and households, schools, clinics, and local forms of political community" that we can reflect critically on what matters and determine how best to live (p. xv). Furthermore, without living "virtuously"—living in a way that engenders generosity of spirit and person—we run the risk of dismantling the importance of asking truly essential questions: "Why?" Why live? Why make music? Why teach and learn anything?

In offering some potential answers to these questions, this volume rests on the premise that the purpose of engagement in/with/through music making—and music teaching and learning—widely seen across a variety of community music sites, programs, and formal school environments—is to engage and pursue lifelong *fulfillment and flourishing* and, in doing so, to live a "good life," a life of meaningfulness and significance (Silverman, 2013). But what does it mean to live a "good life"?

As some of the chapters in this volume propose, the answer to this question involves the concept of ***eudaimonia***. This Greek term derives from "eu," meaning "good" or "well," and "daimon" meaning "a spirit," or "one's personal fortune." Literally, then, it means something like "having a good guardian spirit," or "a good divine power," or "good fortune." Time and again, eudaimonia is translated as "happiness." But, as Gordon Graham (2011) notes, this translation is not very helpful (p. 47). Moreover, interpreting Aristotle, Graham explains that well-being is often "misconceived as mere contentment." Rather, he states, a sense of well-being in this context is exercising "healthy appetites, imaginative and productive use of one's mental faculties, and the establishment of good personal, professional, and public relationships" (pp. 47–48). "Eudaimonia," then, is most often translated as "human flourishing," which requires deeper consideration (Elliott & Silverman, 2014, 2015).

According to Aristotelian ethics, human flourishing and *self-reflective* happiness are the rewards of a life of virtue. Aristotle states, "The human good turns out to be the soul's activity that expresses virtue, and if there is more than one virtue … it will be in a complete life" (*Nicomachean Ethics*, pp. 1098a2, 12–21). As Graham continues, eudaimonia helps to explain the nature of a person's life filled with "active engagement, rather than passive experience" (p. 47). For Aristotle, eudaimonia describes people possessing "excellence," meaning those who live for the betterment of themselves *and their community*, thus maintaining a feeling of contentment, well-being, and comfort. Human flourishing and, thereby, well-being can be achieved when one lives for the betterment of oneself and one's community. This notion of the "good life" and, therefore, "well-being" is at the heart of "artistry" and what it means to rightly live in the world with others (e.g., Wiles, 2016).

Still, commonplace interpretations of eudaimonia—e.g., first-person "happiness" and self-centered flourishing—denote "arguably an ideologically liberal and, indeed, neoliberal stance inherent in [a] eudaimonic lifestyle and philosophy" (Smith, 2016, p. 162). Understanding eudaimonism as concerned only or primarily with seeking purpose and meaning in one's *own* life (Dierendonck & Mohan, 2006; Norton, 1976; Waterman, 1992), while consistent with an ideology pervading certainly the USA and increasingly in other contemporary Western nation states, "contradicts Aristotle's definition of eudaimonia as the fulfillment of one's deepest nature in harmony with the collective welfare" (Della Fave, Brdar, Friere, Vella-Brodrick, & Wissing, 2011, p. 204). Therefore, it is eudaimonism in its fuller, most generous form, for which the authors in this volume advocate. Why? Increased emphasis on individualism and isolation, instead of community and collaboration, can lead to the death of democracy and the rise of narcissists and ignorant populists whose hunger for power threatens to harm millions of people, almost indiscriminately (Levitsky & Ziblatt, 2018). The current fashion for selfishness, myopia, and willful ignorance threatens to undermine the chances of human civilization—in anything like its current forms—surviving at all (Orr, this volume). These pernicious ideologies perpetuated by a powerful few (Giroux, this volume; Sachs, 2019; Wilson & Pickett, 2019) are incredibly challenging, but hopefully not insurmountable obstacles to realizing a more utopian vision for a world guided more by compassion and eudaimonic thriving.

Eudaimonia, Music, and Learning

A belief in the value and pursuit of eudaimonia is called eudaimonism, and we are eudaimonists. We are not advocating for the more selfish version of eudaimonia. Instead, we wish to underline the potential dangers of such a narrow reading and advocate for a more balanced understanding of eudaimonia. We are reminded of bell hooks' (1994) words: that teachers "who embrace the challenge of self-actualization will be better able to create pedagogical practice so that engage students, providing them with ways of knowing that enhance their capacity to live fully and deeply" (p. 22). This seems to strike at the core of the symbiotic eudaimonic dyad—flourishing of oneself *and* of others.

In the contemporary United States where we both reside, such an ideal as that to which Aristotle aspired seems almost unthinkable. People actually flourishing—outside of a consumerist, neoliberal capitalist ideology—is a narrative that runs counter to everything on which contemporary Western societies and national and international power structures are premised. Runaway neoliberalism is defined by the ideas that there is no greater good than the "free" market, and that relentless buying and selling and consuming are the primary purposes of the populace—despite obvious and demonstrated fallacies of "trickle-down" economics and the idea that a few wealthy people will create wealth and better lives for everyone else too, just so long as we all work long and hard enough for them (Chomsky, 1999).

Hannah Arendt (1958) describes market-oriented instrumentalism as meaning that "whatever we do, we are supposed to do for the sake of 'making a living' " (p. 126), and that "not even the 'work' of the artist" is exempt from this logic; "it is dissolved into play and has lost its worldly meaning. The playfulness of the artist is felt to fulfill the same function in the laboring life process of society as the playing of tennis or the pursuit of a hobby fulfills in the life of an individual" (p. 128). Arendt assumes here that the "worldly meaning" of artistry is reification—that art-making, including music-making, somehow transcends the commonplace, the ordinary, the hobby. Such a perspective, however, is at odds with a more holistic eudaimonic view of music(k)ing in which the value of making music is largely in the fulfillment derived from the doing, the process—not in any external value that may be placed on the output (Elliott & Silverman, 2015). Smith (2019), for instance, noted that "rock drumming for me is a particularly autotelic experience. I do it because I need to feel that autotelic experience as part of a meaningful life being me. I do it because it is intrinsically valuable in and of itself" (p. 284). Flourishing in music is possible beyond the canon of "great works" and commercial success.

Since 2012, the United Nations has published several *World Happiness Reports*, looking at "happiness" in ways that align with a eudaimonic notion of well-being as flourishing. One of the 2019 report's authors, Jeffrey D. Sachs, recalls the Easterlin Paradox, noting a negative correlation between GDP increase per capita and reduced subjective well-being among adults in the United States (Easterlin, 1974; Sachs, 2019). He points to three factors likely contributing this situation:

1. "A discrepancy between our evolutionary heritage and our current life conditions" (Sachs, 2019, p. 128), inasmuch as humans have evolved to crave and over-indulge in food when it is available; the over-abundance of foodstuffs today means obesity and associated health risks are very high (Goldman, 2015; Sachs, 2019, p. 128);
2. "High and rising income inequality in high-income societies leads to stress," addiction, and other dysfunctional coping behaviors (Wilkinson & Pickett, 2019); and
3. "A core design feature of a market economy: addictive products boost the bottom line. Americans are being drugged, stimulated, and aroused by the work of advertisers, marketers, app designers, and others who know how to hook people on brands and product lines" (Sachs, 2019, p. 128).

This third hypothesis is supported by another contributing author in the 2019 *World Happiness Report*. Jean M. Twenge discusses a decline in well-being among US American adolescents, which she attributes in large part to massively increased addictive use of digital technologies, primarily via smart phones, and the concomitant reduction in time that people spend together socially, face to face in leisure time. Arendt (1958) also urges us to be wary of finding ourselves with too much leisure time, warning that, left unchecked, humans would greedily fill our free time with endless consumption, leading to a dearth of fulfillment for people and destruction of our planet's resources

(p. 133). We are inclined to be more optimistic than Arendt, though, seeing music(k)ing as a way to flourish without falling prey to the innately human desire to consume.

Active involvement in music-making plays a vital role in many people's leisure time, providing deep fulfillment for people of all ages and abilities, across styles, demographics, and geographies (Mantie & Smith, 2016; Stebbins, 2014). Individuals flourish though personal and communal music making with others who also flourish through these communal activities in contexts that include extreme metal music (Riches, 2016), university marching bands (Weren, Kornienko, Hill, & Yee, 2016), recording studios (Ward & Watson, 2016), Indigenous music-dance (Fox, 2016), video games (O'Leary & Tobias, 2016), YouTube (Cayari, 2016), social media (Trobia & Lo Verde, 2016), and sacred harp singing (Malone, 2016). Active participation in making music can provide "pleasure, relaxation, and an opportunity for self-expression" along with "structure to life … friendships … and spiritual fulfillment" (Hallam, Creech, & Varvarigou, 2016, p. 41). Other manifest benefits of making music include "social networks, a sense of belonging, pride in progress made … with a subsequent impact of self-concept, cognitive, and health benefits" (Hallam, Creech, & Varvarigou, 2016, p. 50); the authors duly note also that any such benefits arising in learning contexts will depend on the quality and qualities of particular teaching and learning experiences.

Not everyone has the luxury or free time in which to undertake leisure activity; the very notion of "leisure" implies privilege. Full-time carers, incarcerated populations, and others may not have time to dedicate to what may seem like frivolous or extraneous activity such as making music. Howell, Higgins, and Bartleet (2016) write about collaborative music-making that is distinct from "more general music-as-leisure." They construe community music as an "'interventionist' mode" of communal music making that works "to enable musical and reflexive responses to the social or health needs of a particular target group, and through this action to cultivate some kind of change or transformation" (p. 605). The ends of such "interventionist" community music, then, align with eudaimonism, especially when we consider that in these settings, skilled facilitators "consciously engage with people to find pathways through which making music might allow them to personally flourish" (p. 605). Furthermore, Lee Higgins (2007) draws on the philosophy of Jacques Derrida to explain how community musicians approach facilitated music-making opportunities as places of "unconditional hospitality" (p. 87). This is a demanding outlook that challenges some assumptions about and approaches to music learning. Without and within formal institutional settings, in music learning contexts of all kinds, teachers, mentors, and facilitators of learning can turn classrooms, studios, rehearsal rooms, and other spaces into *liminal places* of eudaimonic potential for all present (Smith & Shafighian, 2013; Tuan, 1977).

Wealthy countries of the West and the global North provide many of their citizens with ample opportunities to flourish beyond meeting their most basic needs. The financial and material abundance of these dominant nations that affords their inhabitants these life chances, comes at the expense of much poorer countries and the people living in them. Those populations are held in servitude by world powers and the Euro-American businesses that boom in those countries. Indeed, it is precisely such inequity of abundance that means we authors have the luxury of writing this essay and co-editing this volume on a niche philosophical topic in music learning, for a publisher to distribute at a high price-point to a tiny market of people studying for graduate and postgraduate degrees in pedagogy and the arts. Curating this collection has been eudaimonic for us both, but flourishing in music learning need not be so esoteric or abstruse (Smith, 2015).

If power brokers wanted to create a more just world order, in which opportunities and resources were more equitably distributed, they could make that choice. Such a utopia may seem especially unachievable as the United States and other militarily dominant nations strategically shore up their access to the world's finite natural resources in order to maintain their positions atop the world's financial pyramid as they hasten the planet ever faster toward catastrophic climate change. At the very least, though, an orientation toward eudaimonism is arguably at the heart of which it means to be an ethical, loving, compassionate educator, co-learner, student, facilitator, participant, and maker of music. We propose that it is possible to enact and embody this ideal in at least three ways:

1. Understanding that the world is horribly unjust and that recognizing our place in the global system of brutal capitalist plutocracy may help us to envision and act for a more equitable and just world;
2. Taking part in music-making activity that curates mutually flourishing communities where individuals and the collective flourish and thrive and feel the meaningfulness created by and for one another; and
3. Curating spaces for music making, where flourishing through learning is the primary objective.

An ethic of care for others is a vital part of embracing and living eudaimonia. Karin Hendricks' (2018) approach to music learning thus resonates with eudaimonia, as an ethos characterized by "compassion … a relationship of *experience-sharing* in which one might offer support to another based on a shared understanding of feelings, hopes, and/or desires" (p. 5). Higgins (2007), drawing on Lenk (2006), describes communities of music making in which "members are responsible for each other without their personal or individual responsibilities being reduced" (p. 87). David Elliott, Marissa Silverman, and Wayne Bowman (2016) describe something similar, invoking music-making and learning as a form of "*ethically guided citizenship*" (p. 6, emphasis in original), based on the premise that "artistry involves civic-social-humanistic-emancipatory responsibilities, obligations to engage in art making that advances social 'goods'" (Elliott, Silverman, & Bowman, 2016, p. 7). One of the fundamental premises of a eudaimonic orientation is that music and music learning can serve and epitomize human flourishing. The power of music to engender feelings of competence, agency, and community is extraordinary. Music is certainly not uniquely capable in this regard, but we believe, and hope readers may find too, that thinking and acting with eudaimonia is invigorating and exciting.

The notion that each of us should be able to flourish, and not be subject to conditions preventing us from doing so, is a key tenet of anarchism (Bakunin, 1972; Chomsky, 2013; Rocker, 1938). Noam Chomsky (2013) invokes Rudolf Rocker (1938) to explain how contemporary anarchism embraces the eudaimonic dyad of flourishing of the self and others, describing it as the confluence of liberalism and socialism. As a politically motivated, socially conscious alternative construal of educational purpose and praxis, Allan Antliff (2012) describes "anarchist pedagogy" as concerned with "subverting and transcending oppressive social formations" (p. 328). He further explains that:

> Rooted in antiauthoritarian values often at odds with the "mainstream," anarchists conceive of education as a site of critical reflection and creative license, where life and learning comingle, giving rise to ways of being that prefigure and realize our ideals on a practical level, as a lived reality. (p. 326)

In the context of the stifling global neoliberal consensus, "anarchy is the political blank slate of the early twenty-first century. It is shorthand for an eternal now, for a chance to reset the clock" (Schneider, 2013, p. ix). Ruth Wright (2019) considers the implications of anarchism for music learning, rooting her concerns in the need to act to challenge the devastation being wrought on education systems by rampant neoliberalism. Citing Geoffrey Baker (2014), Wright (2019) looks at diverse music-making practices that occur outside of schooling institutions and suggests, "we music-makers might perhaps always have been anarchists at heart and perhaps our mistake has been to try to systematise and codify these practices within education" (p. 221).

All music-making and music-learning practices are to an extent codified and systematized (Cremata, Pignato, Powell, & Smith, 2018; Hebert, Abramo, & Smith, 2017), in order to be recognized *as* practices. Notwithstanding these semantics, it is an alluring conviction – that empowering, agentive, democratic music learning may only be possible in small anarchist communities (inside or outside of schools) that are able to resist the imperatives and pressures of oppressive hegemonic power. Or at least it may be more possible to achieve flourishing—eudaimonia—for individuals and groups in anarchist settings. The idea of anarchist music learning communities recalls the *polis*—the ancient Greek context in which Aristotle defined and for which he envisioned eudaimonia. Perhaps it is not possible for all members of society to thrive in so big and unlikely and diverse a conglomerate as a modern nation state such as the US. Under one flag, people are supposed to share values and ideals but there is such great richness and diversity of wealth, experience, and culture that to suggest we can all thrive under the banner of a nation state is absurd.

The Present Volume

Eudaimonia is an ancient and multifaceted concept, one which includes a variety of virtues—e.g., mindfulness, connectivity, habits, and, importantly, ethics. The concept of eudaimonia is especially pertinent because we live in complicated, contradictory, and frequently uncertain space/time. Whether we're critically reflecting upon our political realities, higher education, or the communities in which we live, it is essential we revisit questions of "why." And even though Steven Pinker (2018) argues that our worlds are better off today than they were years ago, it is still imperative we have answers to larger, ethical questions that should motivate and inform everyday living. We construed this book from the outset to be one that contained perspectives that could provide insight *for* music learning, rather than solely *about* music learning. We were therefore keen to invite thinkers and practitioners from both within the fields of music making and music teaching and learning, but also those beyond these domains of scholarship to interrogate issues surrounding the concept of eudaimonia. Indeed, many valuable insights about "why live" come from outside our fields. Some authors speak more explicitly and at greater length about eudaimonia than others. Our decision to embark on this project was sparked as much by interests in music-making, music-learning and eudaimonia, as by the contemporary socio-political climate in which we live. The world is full of beauty and harmony, while also being violent, dangerous, threatening, terrifying, and unjust. We two alone cannot remake the world for the better, but we felt personally, professionally, and morally obliged to curate a book that framed some of the challenges and potential of eudaimonia.

This book combines perspectives from key contemporary thinkers, who, respectively, consider eudaimonia in conjunction with topics that include music education philosophy, sociology, and spirituality; climate change and the environment; the body, the natural world, the social world, and the cosmic scene; embodiment, community music, and application of theoretical work in collegiate settings and school music classrooms. As such, we aimed to demonstrate how, through eudaimonic music making and music teaching and learning, it is possible to traverse socio-political positionalities that appear increasingly entrenched in the national and international political discourses in which music education takes place. Notably, while eudaimonia is an ancient ethical orientation, it speaks to issues at the core of contemporary life and to the places, purposes, and practicalities of music and music teaching and learning today.

* * *

Dylan van der Schyff describes a recent move from Enlightenment aesthetics and a "technological enframing" of music education toward an increased focus on collaboration and musical activity construed as positive social interaction. van der Schyff explains various ancient Greek understandings of knowledge and ways of being, travelling through *phusis*, *poiesis*, and *ekstasis* before lighting on *phronesis*, which describes a caring disposition. This connects with *orexis*—how humans reach out to the world and to nature to make meaning. The author argues that music learning, conceived as socially oriented musical praxes, is essential to humanity.

The aims and achievements of Jane Addams's Hull House and Hull House Music School provide the springboard for Marissa Silverman's examination of the actual and potential relationships that can be created among music, social ethics, politics, and citizenship. After probing several dimensions of Addams's achievements, her work is considered next to the writings of John Dewey (who was largely influenced by Addams) and several of today's leading feminist theorists. The work of these feminist scholars is especially important in building a more nuanced and balanced understanding of the "ethics of care" that underpinned Addams's musical-communal-ethical work and, today, points us toward a robust concept of democratic school and community music education.

Kathleen Dean Moore's chapter recounts her experiment keeping brief notes over a 12-month period, documenting experiences that made her feel happy. This essay reads as a brief clutch of beautiful, deeply personal recollections, detailing the meaningful, surprising, and mundane. Moore lists things that made her feel truly happy, indicates necessary conditions for enabling these, and lists recurring themes. Overlapping with other chapters in the book, happiness themes including contact with the natural world, stimulating ideas, meaningful work, celebratory arts, and time to pause, reflect, and enjoy. The editors gratefully acknowledge permission granted by Shambhala to reproduce this essay that first appeared in *Wild comfort: The solace of nature* (2010).

Environmentalist David W. Orr discusses the possibility of eudaimonia by reminding readers that the human race is rushing headlong toward catastrophic climate change. Prioritizing consumerism, greed, and isolation, our species is increasingly disconnected from understandings of "biophilia" and "musicophilia" that frame and explain much that is essential to the human condition. Citing community choirs, singing at sports games, and ancient musical mapping of Australia, Orr urges us to position music making far more centrally in our lives and in education policy and practice. With nothing less than the future of our species at stake, music and musicians will play vital roles in securing our collective future.

Cultural critic Henry A. Giroux explores the dehumanization, violence, and racism that characterize a government under the leadership of United States President, Donald Trump. Giroux describes the rise of "neoliberal fascism" threatening the end of democracy in the public imagination in the U.S. Giroux writes of the present as a time of tyranny in which domestic terrorism causes people to lose agency and identity, decrying the role education has played in perpetuating a marketized, consumerist social order. He urges that "it is both a political and pedagogical issue to imagine a future in which human needs take precedent over market considerations," and that the onus is on all educators and artists to act as radical, critical, activist pedagogues.

June Boyce-Tillman traces the history of eudaimonia, from Aristotle's writing of an ethical orientation comprising virtue, wisdom, and flourishing, to its Christianization by Aquinas, who adds the element of transcendence. She argues that self-actualization through music is one of the last remaining places for the soul in Western culture, in which the notion of spirituality has been gradually usurped by aesthetic experience. Boyce-Tillman proposes a phenomenography of music, emphasizing spirituality/liminality and re-engaging with music's connections to the natural world. Like Orr and van der Schyff, this author sees music making as a vital means to challenge the disastrous contemporary socio-political paradigm that burdens and threatens to consume our species; through music we can access spirituality and wonder.

Sophie Haroutunian and Megan Laverty examine Aristotle's conception of eudaimonia as happiness and, as such, as an end in itself. Eudaimonia can be achieved through striving for and achieving excellence, from which people derive pleasure. The authors work with Jean-Luc Nancy's conception of listening as striving to make meaning through what one hears, referring to detailed excerpts from piano lessons between a teacher and an advanced student. They analyze seven segments from the transcription of lesson dialogue identified as moments of listening, and explain how playing music well leads to a more bountiful repertoire of musical meanings, resulting in a greater capacity for happiness through making music. We gratefully acknowledge kind permission of the publisher, G. Henle Verlag, München, to reprint measures 1–58 of Franz Schubert's *Sechs (Six) Moments Musicaux*, Op. 94 – D.780. 1948/1976.

David J. Elliott's chapter concludes this collection by tying together recurring themes from other chapters around the notion of eudaimonia as "well-doing" or ethically guided action. Reiterating the assertion that music making and music learning are integral to human flourishing, Elliott situates a eudaimonic orientation at the heart of music learning. To this end he argues that "effective and ethical music education can make major artistic, social, cultural, gendered, ethical, emotional, mental, and political differences in students' and adults' lives." He discusses obsessions, hedonism, and healthier, harmonious passions. Highlighting the importance of care for self and others, Elliott points to the necessity of love in a life well-lived.

References

Antliff, A. (2012). Let the riots begin. In R. H. Haworth (Ed.), *Anarchist pedagogies: Collective actions, theories, and critical reflections of education*. Oakland, CA: PM Press.

Arendt, H. (1958 [1998]). *The human condition,* 2nd edition. Chicago, IL: University of Chicago Press.

Aristotle. (1985). *Nicomachean ethics*. T. Irwin (Trans.). Indianapolis, IN: Hackett.

Baker, G. (2014). *Orchestrating Venzuela's youth*. Oxford: Oxford University Press.

Bakunin, M. (1972). The program of the alliance. In S. Dolgoff (Ed. & Trans.) *Bakunin on anarchy*, pp. 243–258. New York, NY: Alfred A. Knopf.

Cayari, C. (2016). Music making on YouTube. In R. Mantie & G. D. Smith (Eds.), *The Oxford handbook of music making and leisure*, pp. 467–488. New York, NY: Oxford University Press.

Chomsky, N. (1999). *Profit over people: Neoliberalism and global order*. New York, NY: Seven Stories Press.

Chomsky, N. (2013). *On anarchism*. New York, NY: The New Press.

Cremata, R., Pignato, J., Powell, B., & Smith, G. D. (2018). *The music learning profiles project: Let's take this outside*. New York: Routledge.

Della Fave, A., Brdar, I., Freire, T., Vella-Brodrick, D., & Wissing, M. P. (2011). Eudaimonic and hedonic components of happiness: Qualitative and quantitative findings. *Social Indicators Research*, 100: 185–207.

Dierendonck, D. V., & Mohan, K. (2006). Some thoughts on spirituality and eudaimonic well-being. *Mental Health, Religion and Culture, 9*(3): 227–238.

Easterlin, R. (1974). Does economic growth improve the human lot? Some empirical evidence. In P. A. David & M. W. Reder (Eds.), *Nations and households in economic growth: Essays in honor of Moses Abramovitz*. New York, NY: Academic Press.

Elliott, D. J., & Silverman, M. (2014). Music, personhood, and eudaimonia: Implications for educative and ethical music education. *Journal for Transdisciplinary Research in Southern Africa, 10*(2), 59–74.

Elliott, D. J., & Silverman, M. (2015). *Music matters: A philosophy of music education*, 2nd edition. New York, NY: Oxford University Press.

Elliott, D. J, Silverman, M., & Bowman, W. (2016). Artistic citizenship: Introduction, aims, and overview. In D. J. Elliott, M. Silverman, & W. Bowman (Eds.), *Artistic citizenship: Artistry, social responsibility, and ethical praxis*. New York, NY: Oxford University Press.

Hebert, D., Abramo, J., & Smith, G. D. (2017). Epistemological and sociological issues in popular music education. In G. D Smith, Z. Moir, M. Brennan, S. Rambarran, & P.

Kirkman (Eds.), *The Routledge research companion to popular music education*, pp. 451–477. Abingdon: Routledge.

Fox, K. (2016). Entering into an indigenous cypher: Indigenous music-dance making sings to Western leisure. In R. Mantie & G. D. Smith (Eds.), *The Oxford handbook of music making and leisure*, pp. 519–540. New York, NY: Oxford University Press.

Goldman, L. (2015). *Too much of a good thing*. New York, NY: Little, Brown and Company.

Graham, G. (2011). *Theories of ethics: An introduction to moral philosophy with a selection of classic readings*. New York, NY: Routledge.

Gullotta, & R. Montemayor (Eds.), Adolescent identity formation: Advances in adolescent development. London: Sage.

Hallam, S., Creech, A., & Varvarigou, M. (2016). Well-being and music leisure activities through the lifespan: A psychological perspective. In R. Mantie & G. D. Smith (Eds.), *The Oxford handbook of music making and leisure*, pp. 31–60. New York, NY: Oxford University Press.

Hendricks, K.S. (2018). *Compassionate music teaching. A framework for motivation and engagement in the 21st century*. Lanham, MD: Rowman and Littlefield.

Higgins, L. (2007). *The impossible* future. *Action, Criticism, and Theory for Music Education, 6*(3), 74–96.

hooks, b. (1994). *Teaching to transgress*. New York: Routledge.

Howell, G., Higgins, L., & Bartleet, B.-L. (2016). Community music practice: Intervention through facilitation. In R. Mantie & G. D. Smith (Eds.), *The Oxford handbook of music making and leisure*, pp. 601–618. New York, NY: Oxford University Press.

Lenk, H. (2006). What is responsibility? *Philosophy Now, July/August*: 29–32.

Levitsky, S. & Zibatt, D. (2018). *How democracies die*. New York, NY: Crown.

MacIntyre, A. (2007). *After virtue*. 3rd edition. Notre Dame, IN: University of Notre Dame Press.

Malone, T. (2016). "Singer's music": Considering sacred harp singing as musical leisure and lived harmony. In R. Mantie & G. D. Smith (Eds.), *The Oxford handbook of music making and leisure*, pp. 565–584. New York, NY: Oxford University Press.

Mantie, R. & Smith, G. D. (2016). Grasping the jellyfish of music making and leisure. In R. Mantie & G. D. Smith (Eds.), *The Oxford handbook of music making and leisure*, pp. 3–12. New York, NY: Oxford University Press.

Norton, D. L. (1976). *Personal destinies: A philosophy of ethical individualism*. Princeton, NJ: Princeton University Press.

O'Leary, J. & Tobias, E. S. (2016). Sonic participatory cultures within, through, and around video games. In R. Mantie & G. D. Smith (Eds.), *The Oxford handbook of music making and leisure*, pp. 541–564. New York, NY: Oxford University Press.

Pinker, S. (2018). *Enlightenment now: The case for reason, science, humanism, and progress*. New York, NY: Viking.

Riches, G. (2016). Feeling part of the scene: Affective experiences of music making practices and performances within Leeds's extreme metal scene. In R. Mantie & G. D. Smith (Eds.), *The Oxford handbook of music making and leisure*, pp. 297–318. New York, NY: Oxford University Press.

Rocker, R. (1938). *Anarchosyndicalism*. London: Secker & Warburg.

Sachs, J. D. (2019). Addiction and Unhappiness in America. In J.F. Helliwell, R. Layard, & J. D. Sachs (Eds.), *World happiness report 2019*, pp. 123–121. New York, NY: Sustainable Development Solutions Network.

Schneider, N. (2013). Introduction. In N. Chomsky, *On anarchism*. New York, NY: The New Press.

Silverman, M. (2013). A conception of "meaningfulness" in/for life and music education. *Action, Criticism, and Theory for Music Education*, *12*(2), 20–40. http://act.maydaygroup.org/articles/Silverman12_2.pdf

Smith, G. D. (2015). Neoliberalism and symbolic violence in higher music education. In L. DeLorenzo (Ed.), *Giving voice to democracy: Diversity and social justice in the music classroom*, pp. 65–84 New York, NY: Routledge.

Smith, G. D. (2016). (Un)popular music making and eudaimonism. In R. Mantie & G. D. Smith (Eds.), *The Oxford handbook of music making and leisure*, pp. 151–168. New York, NY: Oxford University Press.

Smith, G. D. & Shafighian, A. (2013). Creative Space and the 'Silent Power of Traditions' in Popular Music Performance Education. In P. Burnard (Ed.), *Developing creativities in higher music education: International perspectives and practices*, pp. 256–267. London: Routledge.

Stebbins, R. A. (2014). Careers in serious leisure: From dabbler to devotee in search of fulfillment. London: Palgrave.

Trobia, A. & Lo Verde, F.M. (2016). Italian amateur pop-rock musicians on Facebook: Mixed methods and new findings in music making research. In R. Mantie & G. D. Smith (Eds.), *The Oxford handbook of music making and leisure*, pp. 489–516. New York, NY: Oxford University Press.

Tuan, Y.-F. (1977). *Space and place: The perspective of experience.* Minneapolis, MN: University of Minnesota Press.

Twenge, J. M. (2019). The sad state of happiness in the United States and the role of digital media. In J. F. Helliwell, R. Layard, & J. D. Sachs (Eds.), *World happiness report 2019*, pp. 87–96. New York, NY: Sustainable Development Solutions Network.

Ward, A. & Watson, A. (2016). "FX, drugs, and rock 'n' roll": Engineering the emotional space of the recording studio. In R. Mantie & G. D. Smith (Eds.), *The Oxford handbook of music making and leisure*, pp. 449–468. New York, NY: Oxford University Press.

Waterman, A. S. (1992). Identity as an aspect of optimal psychological functioning. In G. R. Adams, T. P. Wilkinson, & Pickett, K. (2019). *The inner level: How more equal societies reduce stress, restore sanity and improve everyone's well-being.* New York, NY: Penguin Press.

Weren, S., Kornienko, O., Gary W., Hill, G. W., & Yee, C. (2016). Motivational and social network dynamics of ensemble music making: A longitudinal investigation of a collegiate marching band. In R. Mantie & G. D. Smith (Eds.), *The Oxford handbook of music making and leisure*, pp. 319–343. New York, NY: Oxford University Press.

Wiles, D. (2016). Art and citizenship: The history of a divorce. In D. J. Elliott, M. Silverman, & W. Bowman, (Eds.), *Artistic citizenship: Artistry, social responsibility, and ethical praxis*, pp. 22-40. New York, NY: Oxford University Press.

Wright, R. (2019). Envisioning real Utopias in music education: prospects, possibilities and impediments, *Music Education Research, 21*(3), 217–227.

2 Music Education and the Continuity of Mind and Life

Dylan van der Schyff

For much of the twentieth century, conceptions of music and education were informed by ideas of aesthetics, cognition, and culture received from Enlightenment and Industrial era thinking (Elliott, 1995; Sawyer, 2007). This contributed to a technically-driven pedagogical perspective guided by an understanding of music as a *thing* to be reproduced—and where, accordingly, music education focused on training students to "correctly" analyze and accurately reproduce musical "works" through prescribed modes of practice (Regelski, 2002). In contrast, new approaches highlight the value of more creative, collaborative, and improvisational learning environments. This is inspired by research that explores non-formal contexts for musical development (Green, 2008; Smith, Dines, & Parkinson, 2018); critical reevaluations of what constitutes effective teaching and learning (Kincheloe, 2008); as well as the emergence of interactive and embodied approaches to human cognition (Bowman, 2004; Varela, Thompson, & Rosch, 1991). Additionally, some thinkers have advanced an approach that develops Aristotle's conception of *praxis* as a theoretical framework for guiding thought and action in music education (Elliott & Silverman, 2015; Regelski, 1998). Most centrally, this aptly-named "praxial" approach decenters the focus on the technical abilities associated with the reproduction of pre-existing musical works. While not denying that such skills are important, a praxial turn places more emphasis on the relevance of musical activity for positive forms of personal development and social interaction. It therefore conceives of music education not simply as a kind of training, but rather as an important aspect of what it means to be and become a human being.

In this chapter, I revisit the neo-Aristotelian perspective that informs the praxial approach to music education, connecting the idea of *praxis* more closely with the primordial ontological dimensions associated with biological flourishing and "nature" more generally. I then draw continuities with the increasingly influential orientation in embodied cognitive science referred to as "enactivism." The enactive approach explores the deep continuity between mental processes and biological processes, between mind and life. It therefore offers a radical break from the disembodied and mechanical models that have dominated the Western understanding of mind in the modern era, highlighting the active, situated, and embodied nature of living cognition (Thompson, 2007). To conclude, I consider how a life-based orientation toward mind, music, and education may support the more personally and socially relevant approaches to music education mentioned earlier—how it may offer useful ways of thinking about the meaning of music education and its potential for fostering the forms of "right action" that lead to a eudaimonic existence.[1]

Looking Beyond the Industrial-Technological World View

By the late nineteenth and early twentieth centuries, some thinkers began to warn that our fascination with technological progress was transforming conceptions of being and knowing in ways that could have dire ethical consequences (Husserl, 1970[1936]; Marcuse, 2004[1941]). Such concerns were driven by the observation that as the modern corporate industrial culture adopted a dualistic schema of "man over nature" or "subjects over and against objects," the world was quickly becoming a resource for a global project dedicated to economic growth. This was discussed in terms of the emergence of an impoverished "technologically enframed"[2] ontology (Arendt, 1958; Borgmann, 1984; Dreyfus & Spinosa, 1997; Heidegger, 1977).

Notably, this "technological enframing" does not refer only to the objects of technology that surround us, but also to the ways we position ourselves in the world and how in the modern era we tend to reveal existence to ourselves largely through a mechanistic and instrumental lens. This is reflected, for example, in the consumer culture we all currently live through—where technology becomes not only a product, but also a means to optimize the gathering and processing of resources (both human and "natural"), as well as the distribution and exchange of products within the global economy. The influence of this orientation is also seen in research and theorizing in cognitive science, which for much of the twentieth century understood the mind to be a skull-bound computing machine—downplaying the role of emotion and the living, environmentally situated body for mental life (Damasio, 1994; Varela, Thompson, & Rosch, 1991). Likewise, a technological ontology also guides the depersonalized, bureaucratic, and industrial way education proceeds in the modern world. Here the potentials of students and educators, and the meaning of "education" itself, are often prescribed by externally imposed rules and conventions where "information" is transferred from teacher to student (e.g., the "banking" model; Freire, 2000). This entails a view of education as a kind of mechanical "decontextualized and compartmentalized" (Sawyer, 2007) production line—one where students are trained to memorize and reproduce existing knowledge and to think and perform according to standardized practices; where they study and are tested essentially in isolation; and where teachers are expected to follow pre-given procedures in order to produce pre-determined outcomes that serve the bureaucratic-corporate techno-culture (Giroux, 2011). Here, students and teachers are not conceived of as autonomous creative beings with unique perspectives on the world, but are reduced to part of what Heidegger (1977) refers to as the "standing reserve" (*Bestand*)—future consumers and producers, or indeed, "human resources."[3]

The "bottom line" relevance of music education for this worldview is tenuous at best. As a result, music education advocates have often been reduced to making arguments that confine the meaning and value of music to ends that satisfy the trends of the free-market economy (Elliott & Silverman, 2015). While such advocacy is often well-intentioned, it risks isolating teachers and students in homogenized learning environments and perpetuates the focus on standardized outcomes. It is argued that this orientation divorces musical activity from its relationships with the contingent socio-material contexts that imbue it with meaning for its own sake—that it downplays the active, creative, and improvisatory roles people play in enacting unique musical experiences and relationships; and that it therefore continues to reinforce a depersonalized "technicist" focus in music education.[4]

Notably, a main ethical concern of the *praxial* approach, and current trends in music education more generally, involves understanding and realizing the possibilities music education affords for fostering richer forms of self- and world-making. Accordingly, music education may play a central role in the development of a much needed "ontological pedagogy" that involves a critical reawakening to a more nuanced conception of what human being-in-the-world entails (Kincheloe, 2003). To do this, however, philosophers of music education will need to develop perspectives on the nature and meaning of music—and what it means to be and become a musical being—that decenter the industrial-technological perspective. This requires an approach that does not simply negate our nature as technological beings. Rather, we need to "extend the ontological frame" to reveal the continuities between human being and knowing (including technical varieties) and the emergence and flourishing of living systems more generally.

Revisiting Neo-Aristotelianism for Music Education

As noted earlier, the technological-industrial conception of being need not be understood as the sole possibility for humanity. Rather, it characterizes the world-view of a given historical period. Several twentieth-century philosophers have examined how "being" may be understood in terms of overlapping epochs of human activity, each with its own concerns, beliefs, and activities through which the meaning of existence is disclosed (Dreyfus & Spinosa, 1997; Heidegger, 1977, 2008). In the West, such epochs may be traced through the Roman Empire (with its focus on being as finished works), the rise of Christianity (where being is understood as the creation of a divine God), the Age of Reason and the Enlightenment (the "modern" focus on the "objects" of human reason and progress), and the contemporary industrial and post-industrial world and its preoccupation with economic growth through technological optimization. Here, however, it may be useful to look further back and consider the more primordial conceptions of being and knowing articulated in Ancient Greek thought.

Greek philosophy plays an important role in current music education theorizing, and especially for the neo-Aristotelian praxial perspective mentioned earlier. Here we find what are generally understood as fundamental modes of knowing that can provide more nuanced epistemological frameworks. Such modes are referred to as: (i) *technê* (the technical or procedural knowledge associated with production), (ii) *theoria* (theoretical knowledge), and (iii) *phrónēsis* (situated-embodied or practical-ethical knowledge). To these we may add (iv) *poiesis*, which refers to the activity of production itself and is therefore intimately involved with *technê*. These elements constitute the key components of Aristotle's conception of *praxis*, which concerns the social and ethical forms of activity that initiate positive transformations in the world. Importantly, when a focus on *technê* obscures the other three elements, all connection to *praxis* is lost. In such cases, *technê* is stripped of its ethical responsibility as "technical skills are not, by themselves, individuating, self-actualizing, creative, or personal growth experiences" (Elliott & Silverman, 2015, p. 46).

Taking such insights further, we may develop an even richer conception of praxis by exploring its key components within the "life-based" ontological context mentioned earlier. To do this, we need to consider how the four elements that constitute the Aristotelian conception of *praxis* also have historical origins. Indeed, for the early Greeks the original concern was not with *technê* and *poiesis,* but rather with *phusis.* This term is often translated as "nature," but the concept has more to do with the animate way in which the world was (is) primordially revealed to creatures who "discovered" themselves enmeshed in it (Dreyfus & Kelly, 2011). Indeed, what *being*-as-*phusis* discloses is the way the world (plants, animals, emotions, the weather) continually surges up and transforms. People and things move in and out of existence and other things emerge to take their place; matter and form are enmeshed in an endless process of interactive transformation (one that had best be attended to if survival is to be in any way assured). Importantly, in this context *phusis* is not best understood as an object (something we are over-and-against), nor first and foremost as a kind of "knowledge of," but rather as a mode of "disclosure" in which we are inextricably implicated—the primordial way "being" is revealed by a being who inherently and necessarily *cares* about "being."[5]

It was only later in the sixth and fifth centuries B.C. that the great artisanal culture emerged in Greece and with it the notions of *technê* and *poiesis*. But here again, these concepts cannot be properly understood in modern industrial or postindustrial terms (i.e., instrumentally). Rather, *poiesis* involves a kind of "bringing forth" that is intimately connected with, and develops from, the idea of *phusis*-as-emergence (i.e., the continual surging action of transformation through which the world reveals itself). *Poiesis* may be understood, for example, in terms of *ekstasis,* or how something moves away from its standing as one thing to become another; the unfolding of a thing out of itself (e.g., a plant emerging from a seed), or the emergence of "thingness" from "no-thingness," being from void.[6] However, it may also be conceived of as a kind of nurturing where "things are dealt with as needing to be helped to come forth" (Dreyfus & Spinosa, 1997) as in child rearing, friendship, education, and art-making.

From this perspective, *poieisis* and *phusis* are also inextricably linked. And when they are understood as the active forces/processes behind human forms of making, the idea of *technê* takes on a more nuanced, ethical, and even "sacred" dimension (see Dreyfus & Spinosa, 1997). Here *technê* is revealed as a basic human potential—a fundamental way we reveal our being-in-the-world as creatures who, through our art-making activities, reflect the transformational processes that sustain the world (Heidegger, 1975, 1977).[7] Thus, *technê*-as-*poiesis* may be differentiated from modern "technology" as it involves a disclosing of that good or excellence that is immanently present in the process of production-as-transformation (*ekstasis*).[8] Importantly, the embrace of *technê*-as-*poiesis* involves a renewed appreciation of the sacred nature of *phusis*, where the truth of being may come "shining forth" through the proper cultivation of craft. As Dreyfus and Kelly (2011) argue, the *meta-poietic* mode of being associated with the artist, musician, or craftsperson is therefore something all human beings must strive for if they are to achieve true authenticity and a flourishing existence—or in a word, *eudaimonia.*

It is also important to reassert that the life movements and dispositions associated with the forms of ontological disclosure involved with *praxis* are underpinned by a primordial *caring* attitude toward the world—a fundamentally affective-emotional way of being that characterizes human life (Colombetti, 2014). This caring attitude is the essence of *phrónēsis,* which refers to how the possibilities of our contingent existence are revealed through meaningful action. For Aristotle, *phrónēsis* concerns our direct involvement with life, most fundamentally the concern for survival and well-being (of ourselves and others) that forms the background to our existence. As such, *phrónēsis* may be understood as the primordial disposition for human meaning making—the fundamental way human worlds are revealed through the transformative and embodied (inter)activity (the life-movements) associated with the idea of *praxis*. In all, *phrónēsis* describes how we engage in the deliberative ethical action that is relevant to the contingencies of the moment; how we reach out to the socio-material environments we inhabit and thus project certain possibilities "ahead of ourselves" within a changing world. In this way, *phrónēsis* may be understood as a reflection of *phusis* in human world-making; and is, therefore, the ground and guide to all other modes of *praxis* (*technê, poiesis, theoria*).

Considering *praxis* from this life-based ontological perspective deepens our understandings of what knowledge, meaning, and being entail. It aligns them more closely with the fundamental embodied-social processes through which we open to the possibilities of being-in-the-world as we strive toward a flourishing existence. Interestingly, these processes also characterize the experience of music—not first and foremost as an object of thought or reproduction, but rather as something we live through with our whole being as the emotional and empathic creatures we are. Such insights resonate closely with recent embodied or so-called "enactive" approaches to cognition (Thompson, 2007). Therefore, the integration of praxial and enactive perspectives may offer important insights into how and why music is meaningful for human existence when it conceives of (musical) cognition not first in terms of detached rational processes and dualistic mechanistic analogies (i.e., the mind as computer), but rather as deeply continuous with the most basic operations of life itself (van der Schyff, 2015a).

Mind-in-Life: The Enactive Perspective

Enactivism is an interdisciplinary field that explores cognition across a wide range of areas including neuroscience, social-cognition, developmental studies, philosophy of mind, phenomenology, theoretical biology, linguistics, education, and music (Stewart, Gapenne, & Di Paolo, 2010). Centrally, the enactive approach asserts the deep continuity between mind and life, where cognition (including its emotional-affective dimensions) is understood most fundamentally as *perceptually guided action* (Nöe, 2006). Accordingly, a meaningful world is brought forth (or "enacted") through the continuous interactivity between organism and environment—where mind is understood as a main property of this dynamically evolving organism-environment system. By this light, mind, body, and world are inseparable; cognition is necessarily embodied and environmentally situated.

To better understand the relationships between enactivism and the ontological perspective discussed earlier, it is useful to introduce yet another of Aristotle's ideas—albeit one that receives very little attention in the philosophical literature. Notably, his notion of *orexis* (2001; see *De Anima*) describes the essentially striving or conative nature of living beings; the way organisms "reach out" to the world to sustain themselves and develop their potential as fully as possible. *Orexis* is often referred to as "desire." However, as philosopher Martha Nussbaum (2001) points out, this term has much richer developmental, ethical, and spiritual implications than the word desire might imply. Nussbaum discusses *orexis* in the context of human life by describing how we reach out to the world (to nature, things, our parents and siblings, our friends and colleagues, our society, other societies) with our bodies, senses, minds and souls to understand (to feel, intuit, imagine, and rationalize) our needs, desires, reasons, and conditions, and thereby engage in the process of enacting the worlds we inhabit. As she explains, "we all [natural beings] reach out, being incomplete, for things in the world. That is the way our movements are caused" (p. 289). It is important to note here that the notion of *orexis* casts even the most basic forms of living world-making first in terms of active embodied engagements with the world as opposed to responses. It therefore highlights the primarily "goal directed" nature of living systems in their *movements toward* flourishing.

This last point reveals an important Aristotelian (2001; see *Phys. II*) distinction between the ontological status of the "natural" and the "artificial"—or the "living" and the "made." This distinction allows us to see that, whereas the products of technology (the things people make) have their ontological footing outside of themselves, nature (*phusis*) is essentially "self-moving," "self-revealing," or *autopoietic* (self-producing or self-organizing).[9] The modern computer provides an excellent example. While a computer can be said to perform cognitive functions, it has no access to what those functions could mean. A computer's functioning as an information-processor necessarily remains wholly dependent on the outside entities (i.e., humans) who input data, who impose meaning on outputs, and who bring it into being in the first place. Its existence is therefore non-autonomous and thus non-caring (*non-phrónētic*). A computer's coming-into-being and the meaning of its existence are determined externally. At best, a computer can only give an illusion of the relational activity we find between autonomously interacting *living* systems (Dreyfus, 1992).

Living creatures, by contrast, are intrinsically meaningful. They move themselves into existence and *actively* and *autonomously* participate in the construction and maintenance of their own life-worlds. They open (disclose) unique ecologies of salience, which are informed by their interactions with every form of "otherness" they may meet. To achieve and maintain a viable existence, *living* cognitive systems must exhibit "operational closure." This refers to their autonomous identity instantiated most fundamentally in the bounded metabolic, self-regulative processes necessary for an organism to be differentiated as such (Di Paolo, 2005; Varela, 1979). However, a living being must also simultaneously maintain the dynamic organism-environment *interactivity* that allows it to "make-sense" of its world in relation to its intrinsic needs (Barbaras, 2010). This necessary co-arising asymmetry between autonomous, self-generating (closed) metabolic processes and the (open) sensorimotor dynamics of "sense-making" may be observed in even the most basic single celled organisms—which, while not possessing the complex neural structures to support explicitly representational forms of cognition, are nevertheless capable of engaging in the kinds of active and conative-valenced behaviors necessary to enact viable relationships with their environment and thereby realize an adaptive "point of view" (a primordial "self") (Thompson, 2007). Such insights have led a growing number of researchers to argue that we should no longer base our conceptions of cognition in technological metaphors (i.e., the mind as computer), but rather examine mind as ontologically continuous with the fundamental biological processes of life itself.[10]

This life-based turn lies at the heart of the so-called enactive approach—which, as I considered earlier, argues that living cognition involves an ongoing process of *action-as-perception*; a circular process of contingent organism-environment interactivity whereby a meaningful world is continually and actively brought forth (Di Paolo, Buhrmann, & Barandiaran, 2017). Among other things, this perspective reconsiders notions of "knowledge" and "information," not as things to be acquired, but rather in terms of developmental processes. In other words, information is not objectively "out there" in a pre-given world waiting to be processed by an anonymous subject; meaning and knowledge are not "generated," "computed" nor simply abstractly represented in the head. Rather, an enactive ontology reveals that meanings are emergent phenomena that depend on the self-organizing or self-making (*autopoiesis*) processes of the whole creature as it enacts a meaningful world through a history of interaction with the environment. Meaning is thus impossible to reduce to objective inner or outer structures (Varela, Thompson, & Rosch, 1991). Moreover, because such basic forms of sense-making are inherently embodied, adaptive, conative, and valenced (i.e., "caring"), cognition and emotion are no longer understood as separate domains, but rather as deeply continuous with one another (Colombetti, 2014).

Of course, sense-making can involve much more than the basic metabolic dimensions described earlier. Indeed, human self- and world-making (*autopoiesis*) entail a lived history of social embodiment through which meaningful interpersonal and cultural ecologies emerge and evolve (Johnson, 2007). This necessarily involves the development of various skills and ways of thinking, as well as participatory forms of sense making whereby multiple agents bring forth shared worlds of meaning (De Jaegher & Di Paolo, 2007). This insight resonates rather closely with the fundamental mode of human being-in-the-world associated with *phrónēsis* and the active and caring relationship with being it describes. It also returns us to the notions of *poietic technê* and *theoria* to consider how such distinctly human modes of existential disclosure are continuous with the primordial concepts of *autopoiesis* and *orexis* common to all life forms. Again, from this perspective the "categories" associated with the notion of *praxis* are not best understood as discrete domains of knowledge, but rather as mutually influencing dispositions that drive the manifold life movements through which we enact meaningful relationships with the world. An important implication of this perspective is that it offers a view of musicality that is continuous with biological existence —where music is seen as a primary way the human animal actively reaches out to and interacts with the socio-material environment, and thereby brings forth a world that is relevant to its well-being.

Human Being as Musical Being

Musical experience surges up and transforms, and this involves the emergence of various feelings, emotions, and shifting relationships, as well as experiences of movement and space (Johnson, 2007). Musical experience is also deeply embodied and inextricable from the socio-material environment. We engage with music—through listening and performing—not as passive responders, but rather through active relational, adaptive, creative, and indeed, "improvisational" processes whereby musical worlds are brought forth and sustained (Clarke, 2005; van der Schyff, 2019). As already noted, this is a *poietic* process that reflects the transformational nature of *phusis.* However, the enactment of musical experience is also primordially "phronetic" as it necessarily engages our empathic and caring capacities—it entails a concern for the relationships between ourselves and the others involved (co-performers, audience members, and so on) (Clarke, 2018; Silverman, 2012).[11]

Among other things, a conception of musicality as deeply continuous with the fundamental dimensions of human being and knowing offers an alternative to the commodifying tendencies of the current prevailing consumer culture. As scholars (Elliott & Silverman, 2015; Lines, 2003) have noted, the modern understanding of music has often been framed in "nihilistic" terms— where music is assumed to be an essentially meaningless pleasure technology (or product) that has little relevance to the day-to-day and evolutionary concerns related to our survival and well-being (e.g., see Pinker, 1997). This assumption is now questioned by research that examines the centrality of music for human life in other social and cultural environments; from studies that explore the importance of music in therapeutic contexts; as well as the growing interest in how people actually engage with music in a range of contexts in everyday life (Blacking, 1995; DeNora, 2000; Small, 1998). Musicality also plays a crucial role in the development of the emotional and social scaffolding that affords interpersonal cohesion (Krueger, 2013, 2014)—the very grounding of *phrónēsis* and personhood. This involves the development of pre-linguistic aesthetic modes of communication and understanding that enable the forms of adaptive "primary intersubjectivity" between infants and caregivers necessary for developing social bonds (Trevarthern, 2002).

From enactive perspectives, such embodied-affective "aesthetic" processes are understood to ground and motivate the kinds of social "participatory sense-making" (De Jaegher & Di Paolo, 2007; Johnson, 2007) that we continue to engage in throughout our lives. This reveals musicality as a paradigmatic example of the interactive "relational autonomy" that lies at the heart of the enactive approach to social cognition.[12] It highlights the socially extended and improvisational nature of the human (musical) mind as it evolves "dynamically in the relationship between organisms and their surroundings (including other agents)" (McGann, De Jaegher, & Di Paolo, 2013). In all, this perspective reveals human musicality not simply in terms of pre-given sets of knowledge and behaviors that are to be reproduced. Rather, it is shown as an adaptive, participatory, and empathic phenomenon—a form of (social) sense-making that involves the enactment of shared patterns of action and perception that continuously shape and renew a shared cognitive ecology.[13]

As an example of this we might consider the self-organizing dynamics of an interacting musical ensemble (e.g., a jazz trio or a string quartet). In such contexts, the musicians involved must adaptively engage with the manifold and transforming relationships that arise in the enactment of a musical event —these include corporeal, material, emotional, and aesthetic-cultural dimensions that are distributed throughout the musical environment. Importantly, the forms of embodied agent-environment interactivity associated with such processes are continuous with the fundamental forms of active (participatory) sense-making just discussed, where agents co-enact, and work to maintain, a shared environment (Schiavio & van der Schyff, 2018). In this way, the co-creation of musical worlds also involves a re-engagement with the experience of *phusis* and *poiesis*, affording an opportunity for these primary dimensions of being to "shine forth" through musical *praxis.* Here, advanced technical skills and theoretical knowledge are not ends unto themselves. Instead, they serve to maintain, develop, and *nurture* the self-organizing dynamics of musical activity.

From an enactive perspective, then, human musicality is far more than a pleasure technology (or "auditory cheesecake"; Pinker, 1997); music cannot be reduced to technical processes associated with the reproduction and consumption of musical works and products. Rather, it is central to human well-being as one of the principal ways we orient ourselves relationally in the world as dynamic self-makers who span physical, biological, emotional, socio-cultural, rational-technical, and theoretical modes of being. Here music-as-*praxis* is also revealed as continuous with the notion of *orexis* and *phrónēsis*—a central way human beings actively reach out to the world, form environments for each other, and thereby reveal or enact shared worlds of meaning. It follows, then, that our (embodied-aesthetic) musical nature is central to what it means to be and become a person when it affords a harmonious integration of the multiple modes of being-in-the-world available to us as the *autonomous*, *autopoietic,* and fundamentally *caring* social beings we are.

Conclusion

The ontological perspective sketched here supports current alternatives to music pedagogies tacitly informed by a commodifying, dehumanizing, and technically-driven worldview. Accordingly, this orientation is also a critical one when it allows us to better see how some modern approaches impose views of mind, music, and education that obscure essential aspects of what human being and becoming can entail; how this is primordially unethical when it wrenches away the active, transformative, and self-revealing nature of human-being-as-musical-being, turning the natural into the artificial; and how this reduces the ontological status of students and teachers, forcing them to passively comply with externally driven standards. In doing so, a life-based enactive music pedagogy asks us to critically reengage with fundamental questions: What is music? What is education? What is a musical mind? A self? A person? A flourishing life? An important implication of this is that it demands a new conception of what being and becoming an "educator" entails. By this light, he or she is no longer simply a repository of facts and information. Rather, the educator becomes one who embodies learning—one who, through action, discloses the *praxis* of education as an opening up to the world and who strives to help students reach their *autopoietic* (self-making) potentials as master learners themselves. Here the educator is revealed as an artist in the nurturing, *poietic* sense discussed earlier—where pedagogical "craft" (*technê*) is directed toward revealing musical learning as a manifestation of human self- and world-making.

Gaining a deeper understanding of the fundamentally embodied, social, and ecological grounding for human being and knowing is central to new critically ontological approaches to education (Kincheloe, 2003; 2008; Thomson, 2001; van der Schyff, Schiavio, & Elliott, 2016). These begin with the recognition and clearing away of assumptions that obscure the essence of being, so that other possibilities may come forth:

> [A] critical ontology positions the body in relation to cognition and the process of life itself. The body is a corporeal reflection of the evolutionary concept of autopoiesis, self-organizing, or self-making of life. If life is self-organized, then there are profound ontological, cognitive, and pedagogical implications. By recognizing new patterns and developing new processes, humans exercise much more input into their own evolution than previously imagined. In such a context, human agency and possibility is enhanced.
>
> (Kincheloe, 2003, p. 50)

Once the modern technological-industrial ontology is critically decentered, music and education may show themselves as the embodied life-movements they are—as participatory and transformational "focal practices" through which the possibilities of being may "shine forth" and whereby the world may be cast in a new light (Borgmann, 1984; Dreyfus & Spinosa, 1997). Among other things, this shift may reveal continuities between aspects of being that often seem dichotomous in the modern world: self and other; mind and body; emotion and reason; nature and culture; technology and human authenticity. Accordingly, the life-based perspectives found in Ancient Greek thought and the enactive approach to cognition may offer important ontological and ethical groundings for new pedagogies that seek to encourage human flourishing through creative musical *praxis.*

Acknowledgements

This chapter is based on an earlier paper (van der Schyff, 2015b) that appeared in *Action, Criticism, and Theory for Music Education.* I thank the journal for permission to reuse and rework sections of this article in the present chapter. This chapter also develops ideas originally introduced in three other papers (van der Schyff, 2010; van der Schyff, 2015a; van der Schyff, Schiavio, & Elliott, 2016). My appreciation goes to the editors of this volume for the opportunity to revisit this material and reframe it in a way that, I hope, is more coherent and useful for the field of music education.

Notes

1. Elliott and Silverman (2015) write that engagements with musics "trace back to the fundamental issue of what it means to be the kind of living entity that possesses, undergoes, enacts and 'performs' his or her personhood" (p. 154).
2. Heidegger (1977) introduced the term "Gestell" to refer to this.
3. As Elliott and Silverman (2015) note, "The overriding concern of neoliberal education emphasizes producing workers fit for the short-term needs of global business" (p. 119). Similarly, Dreyfus (2002) notes the world "has become 'a system of information' and a modern airliner is not an object at all, but just a flexible and efficient cog in the transportation system. Passengers are presumably not autonomous subjects either, but resources recruited by the tourist industry to fill the planes" (page n/a). As Lines (2003) states, music is often framed in this commodifying light—as a resource to be exploited for economic ends.
4. Bowman (2004) warns that when music education proceeds in this way it obscures music's "participatory, enactive, and embodied character" as well as its capacity to "highlight the co-origination of body, mind, and culture" (p. 46).
5. Heidegger (2008) uses the term "Dasein" to refer to such beings.
6. Abbs (1994) explains that education is "an opening out of the mind that transcends detail and skill and whose movement cannot be predicted ... the expression of a primary impulse for truth, a deep epistemic instinct that we inherit as part of our biological nature" (pp. 15–16). This aligns with core insights in Eastern thinking (see Nakagawa, 2000; van der Schyff, 2015a).
7. This is echoed by Kohák (1984): "[Technology] is not only a convenience but also an authentic human possibility [... The human being] is an artificer not by accident

but essentially. [...] If the products of human *technê* become philosophically and experientially problematic it is ... because we come to think of them as autonomous of the purpose which led to their production and give them meaning" (pp. 23–24).

8. Likewise, the development of *theoria* may be understood not simply as a kind of knowing, but also as a fundamental movement of human life-as-thought toward normative principles that guide action and understanding (yet another mode of "revealing" or "disclosing" the world). Notably, the emergence of theory with Plato and the sophists also marks a turning point away from *phusis* and the *poietic* world view (see Dreyfus, 2002).
9. The term "autopoiesis" was originally developed in the realm of theoretical biology by Maturana and Varela (1980). It refers to the self-organizing (or literally, self-making) and thereby autonomous nature of living organisms.
10. Such insights resonate with Dewey's (1991) principle of continuity where, "rational operations grow out of organic activities, without being identical with that from which they emerge" (p. 26).
11. Philosophers Johnson (2007) and Sheets-Johnstone (1999), and neuroscientist Ramachandran (2011) argue the embodied-affective forms of meaning-making associated with music (and other expressive activities such as painting and dance) are indicative of a basic non- or pre-linguistic cross-modal aesthetic capacity that grounds all forms of cognition—ways of knowing that emerge from our histories as embodied-affective beings who strive toward meaning in our interactions with the social, material, and cultural environments we live through.
12. Enactive "relational autonomy" is characterized by its "extended" and interactive nature, as opposed to detached Enlightenment notions where autonomous agents are assumed to be "primordially lone individuals extending their cognitive reach" (Urban, 2014, p. 4; De Jaegher, 2013).
13. The improvisational nature of living cognition is also highlighted by Varela and colleagues (1991) who state that the mind involves adaptive and embodied learning, which is not simply knowledge of "this" or "that," but rather "knowing how to negotiate our way through a world that is not fixed and pre-given but that is continually shaped by the types of actions in which we engage" (p. 144). With reference to music, see Torrance and Schumann, 2018.

References

Abbs, P. (1994). *The educational imperative: A defense of Socratic and aesthetic learning.* London: Falmer Press.

Arendt, H. (1958). *The human condition.* Chicago, IL: University of Chicago Press.

Aristotle. (2001). *The basic works of Aristotle.* Edited by Richard McKeon. New York: Modern Library.

Barbaras, R. (2010). Life and exteriority: The problem of metabolism. In J. Stewart, O. Gapenne & E. A. Di Paolo (Eds.), *Enaction: Toward a new paradigm for cognitive science,* (pp. 89–122). Cambridge, MA: The MIT Press.

Blacking, J. (1995). *Music, culture and experience.* London: University of Chicago Press.

Borgmann, A. (1984). *Technology and the character of contemporary life: A philosophical inquiry.* Chicago: University of Chicago Press.

Bowman, W. D. (2004). Cognition and the body: perspectives from music education. In L. Bresler (Ed.), *Knowing bodies, moving minds: Toward embodied teaching and learning,* (pp. 29–50). Netherlands: Kluwer Academic Press.

Clarke, E. F. (2005). *Ways of listening: An ecological approach to the perception of musical meaning.* Oxford: Oxford University Press.

Clarke, E. F. (2018). Empathy and the ecology of musical consciousness. In D. Clarke, R. Herbert & E. F. Clarke (Eds.), *Music and Consciousness II* (pp. 71–92). Oxford University Press.

Colombetti, G. (2014). *The feeling body: Affective science meets the enactive mind.* Cambridge, MA: MIT Press.

Damasio, A. (1994). *Descartes' error: Emotion, reason and the human brain.* New York: Random House.

De Jaegher, H. (2013). Rigid and fluid interactions with institutions. *Cognitive Systems Research,* 25, 19–25. doi: 10.1016/j.cogsys.2013.03.002

De Jaegher, H., & Di Paolo, E. (2007). Participatory sense-making: An enactive approach to social cognition. *Phenomenology and the Cognitive Sciences, 6*(4), 485–507. https://doi.org/10.1007/s11097-007-9076-9

DeNora, T. (2000). *Music in everyday life.* Cambridge: Cambridge University Press.

Dewey, J. (1938/1991). Logic: The theory of inquiry. In A. Boydston (Ed.), *John Dewey: The later works, 1925–1953* (Vol. 12). Carbondale, IL: SIU Press.

Di Paolo, E. A. (2005). Autopoiesis, adaptivity, teleology, agency. *Phenomenology and the Cognitive Sciences, 4*(4): 429–52. doi:10.1007/s11097- 005–9002-y

Di Paolo, E. A., Buhrmann, T., & Barandiaran, X. (2017). *Sensorimotor life: An enactive proposal.* New York: Oxford University Press.

Dreyfus, H. (1992). *What computers still can't do: A critique of artificial reason.* Cambridge, MA: MIT Press.

Dreyfus, H., & Spinosa, C. (1997). Highway bridges and feasts: Heidegger and Borgmann on how to affirm technology. *Proceedings of the Conference on After Postmodernism.* www.focusing.org/apm_papers/dreyfus.html

Dreyfus, H. (2002). Being and power: Heidegger and Foucault. http://people.ischool.berkeley.edu/~dilanm/ieor/being.power_hubert.dreyfus.pdf

Dreyfus, H., & Kelly, S. D. (2011). *All things shining: Reading Western classics to find meaning in a secular age.* New York: Simon and Schuster.

Elliott, D. J. (1995). *Music matters: A new philosophy of music education.* New York: Oxford University Press

Elliott, D. J., & Silverman, M. (2015). *Music matters: A philosophy of music education* (2nd ed.). New York: Oxford University Press.

Freire, P. (2000). *Pedagogy of the oppressed.* New York: Continuum International Publishing Group.

Giroux, H. (2011). *On critical pedagogy.* New York: Continuum.

Green, L. (2008). *Music, informal learning and the school: A new classroom pedagogy.* London: Ashgate Press.

Heidegger, M. (1975). *Poetry, language, thought.* New York: Harper Perennial.

Heidegger, M. (1977). The question concerning technology. In *The question concerning technology and other essays* (pp. 3–35). New York: Garland Publishing.

Heidegger, M. (2008). *Being and time.* New York: Harper Collins.

Husserl, E. (1970/1936). *The crisis of European sciences and transcendental philosophy.* Evanston, IL: Northwestern University Press.

Johnson, M. (2007). *The meaning of the body: Aesthetics of human understanding.* Chicago, IL: University of Chicago Press.

Kincheloe, J. L. (2003). Critical ontology: Visions of selfhood and curriculum. *Journal of Curriculum Theorizing, 19*(1), 47–64.

Kincheloe, J. L. (2008). *Knowledge and critical pedagogy: An introduction.* London: Springer.

Kohák, E. (1984). *The embers and the stars.* Chicago, IL: University of Chicago Press.

Krueger, J. (2013). Empathy, enaction, and shared musical experience. In T. Cochrane, B. Fantini & K. Scherer (Eds.), *The emotional power of music: Multidisciplinary perspectives on musical expression, arousal, and social control* (pp. 177–196). New York: Oxford University Press.

Krueger, J. (2014). Affordances and the musically extended mind. *Frontiers in psychology, 4*, 1003. doi:10.3389/fpsyg.2013.01003

Lines, D. (2003). Blacking's legacy: The transformational and affective dimension of music education. Paper presented at the Blacking Symposium, University of Western Australia, July 2003. Retrieved from www.academia.edu/3088750/Blacking_s_Legacy_The_Transformational_and_Affective_Dimension_of_Music_Education

Marcuse, H. (2004/1941). Some social implications of modern technology. In D. Kellner (Ed.), *Technology, war and fascism: Collected papers of Herbert Marcus* (pp. 138–162). London: Routledge.

Maturana, H., & Varela F. J. (1980). *Autopoiesis and cognition: The realization of the living.* Dordrecht, NL: Reidel Publishing.

McGann, M., De Jaegher, H., & Di Paolo. E. A. (2013). Enaction and psychology. *Review of General Psychology, 17*(2), 203–209. doi:10.1037/a0032935

Nakagawa, Y. (2000). *Education for awakening: An Eastern approach to holistic education.* Brandon, VT: Education Renewal.

Nöe, A. (2006). *Action in perception.* Cambridge, MA: MIT Press.

Nussbaum, M. C. (2001). *The fragility of goodness.* New York: Cambridge University Press.

Pinker, S. (1997). *How the mind works.* New York: Norton.

Ramachandran, V. S. (2011). *The tell-tale brain: A neuroscientist's quest for what makes us human.* New York: Norton.

Regelski, T. A. (1998). The Aristotelian bases of praxis for music and music education as praxis. *Philosophy of Music Education Review, 6*(1), 22–59.

Regelski, T. A. (2002). On "methodolatry" and music teaching as critical and reflective praxis. *Philosophy of Music Education Review, 10*(2), 102–123.

Sawyer, K. R. (2007). Improvisation and teaching. *Critical Studies in Improvisation, 2*(2). Retrieved from www.criticalimprov.com/article/view/380/626

Schiavio, A., & van der Schyff, D. (2018). 4E music pedagogy and the principles of self-organization. *Behavioral Sciences*, *8*(8), 72. Retrieved from https://doi.org/10.3390/bs8080072

Sheets-Johnstone, M. (1999). *The primacy of the movement.* Amsterdam: John Benjamins.

Silverman, M. (2012). Virtue ethics, care ethics, and "the good life of teaching". *Action, Criticism, and Theory for Music Education, 11*(2), 96–122.

Small, C. (1998). *Musicking: The meaning of performing and listening.* Middletown, CT: Wesleyan UP.

Smith, G. D., Dines, M., & Parkinson, T. (Eds.). (2018). *Punk pedagogies: Music, culture and learning.* New York: Routledge.

Stewart, J., Gapenne, O., & Di Paolo, E. A. (Eds.). (2010). *Enaction: Toward a new paradigm for cognitive science.* Cambridge, MA: MIT Press.

Thompson, E. (2007). *Mind in life: Biology, phenomenology and the sciences of mind.* Cambridge, MA: Harvard University Press.

Thomson, I. (2001). Heidegger on ontological education, or: How we become what we are. *Inquiry, 44*(3), 243–268.

Torrance, S., & Schumann, F. (2018). The spur of the moment: What jazz improvisation tells cognitive science. *AI & Society, 34*(2), 1–18. Retrieved from https://doi.org/10.1007/s00146-018-0838-4

Trevarthern, C. (2002). Origins of musical identity: Evidence from infancy for musical social awareness. In R. R. MacDonald, D. J. Hargreaves & D. Miell (Eds.), *Musical Identities* (pp. 21–38). Oxford: Oxford University Press.

Urban, P. (2014). Toward an expansion of an enactive ethics with the help of care ethics. *Frontiers in Psychology, 5*, 1354. doi:10.3389/fpsyg.2014.01354

van der Schyff, D. (2010). The ethical experience of nature: Aristotle and the roots of ecological phenomenology. *Phenomenology and Practice, 4*(1), 97–121.

van der Schyff, D. (2015a). Music as a manifestation of life: Exploring enactivism and the "eastern perspective" for music education. *Frontiers in Psychology, 6*, 345. doi:10.3389/fpsyg.2015.00345

van der Schyff, D. (2015b). Praxial music education and the ontological perspective: An enactivist response to *Music Matters 2. Action, Criticism, and Theory for Music Education, 14*(3): 75–95.

van der Schyff, D., Andrea S., & David E. (2016). Critical ontology for an enactive music pedagogy. *Action, Criticism, and Theory for Music Education, 15*(5), 81–121.

van der Schyff, D. (2019). Improvisation, enaction, and self-assessment. In D. J. Elliott, M. Silverman & G. McPherson (Eds.), *The Oxford handbook of philosophical and qualitative perspectives on assessment in music education* (pp. 319–346), New York: Oxford University Press.

Varela, F. J. (1979). *Principles of biological autonomy.* New York: North Holland.

Varela, F. J., Thompson, E., & Rosch, E, (1991). *The embodied mind: Cognitive science and human experience.* Cambridge, MA: MIT Press.

3 The Hull House

A Case Study in Eudaimonia for Music Learning

Marissa Silverman

Scholars across various domains have explored the "good" work of Chicago's Hull House, a settlement established in 1889 by young women to assist various needs—emotional, spiritual, educational, social, and more—of working-class immigrants. However, the music education community has not given the Hull House the attention it deserves. Only a few sources of music education and community music scholarship take notice of its significance (e.g., Allsup & Shieh, 2012; Elrod, 2001; Howe, 2013); others tangentially mention its contributions (e.g., Volk, 1998; Laird, 2009; Leglar & Smith, 2010; Vogel, 2013).

Therefore, this chapter focuses on the Hull House to provide the springboard for an examination of relationships that can be created among music and social ethics, or, in other words, *eudaimonia for music learning*. Doing so is important in building a nuanced and balanced understanding of the "ethics of care" (e.g., Noddings, 2003; Slote, 2007) that underpinned Jane Addams's —one of Hull House's founders, and the second woman to receive the Nobel Peace Prize in 1931[1]—musical-communal-ethical work and, today, points us toward a robust concept of democratic and eudaimonic school and community music education.

What follows provides a brief introduction about the natures and values of eudaimonia. Additionally, this chapter illustrates details about Hull House's founders, Jane Addams and Ellen Gates Starr, as well as the Hull House itself.[2] In doing so, readers will find connections among the Hull House, the progressive era, and the scholarship of John Dewey. These discussions are linked to an ethic of care (e.g., Held, 2006; Hoagland, 1991; Jaggar, 1995; Kittay Feder & Meyers, 1987; Noddings, 2010). Lastly, concluding thoughts highlight implications for music teaching and learning.

Eudaimonia

In ancient Greece—as explained in my co-authored chapter (Silverman & Elliott, 2016) in the edited volume, *Artistic Citizenship*—all artistic practices were grouped under the concept, *mousikê*. *Mousikê* denotes a wide range of social, religious, and educational activities, including singing, dancing, poetry, storytelling, mythology, and rhythm and melody accompanied by gestures and poses performed by amateur actors (Wright, 1969, pp. 37–41; Murray & Wilson, 2004). Thus, *mousikê* is not isolated onto itself, as the concept "music" tends to be understood in the West. *Mousikê* is a concept that explains the integrated and interconnected nature—a union—of all arts practices as expressed within particular contexts.

Most notably, and because of the multidimensional nature of the practices involved, *mousikê* served as the foundation for ancient Greek education (Murray & Wilson, 2004), and thus an integral part of the Greek concept of *paideia*. *Paideia*, or character and civic education, involved the processes that help individuals become positively useful to themselves and to the polis, which includes one's family, friends, and community. At the core of paideia is an

> all-round civic education that involves a life-long process of character development, absorption of knowledge and skills and—more significant—practicing a "participatory" kind of active citizenship, that is a citizenship in which political activity is not seen as a means to an end but an end in itself.
>
> (Fotopoulos, 2003, p. 17)

On this view, "thriving" fuses self and society (Silverman & Elliott, 2016), the aim of which is a flourishing social system or ecology. Following this, individuals seek out opportunities to be the "best" versions of themselves for the good of self, community, and the world around them. Thus, the goal of paideia, "*is not mastery of subject matter, but of one's person*" (Orr, 2004, italics in original, p. 13). How does such "mastery" get acquired? According to Aristotle, people only develop themselves fully through active and thoughtful participation in the social practices and activities of the polis. As individuals learn and embody the habits and characteristics of excellence, so will the polis become more virtuous and excellent (Crittenden & Levine, 2013).

As Aristotle states in *Nicomachean Ethics*, a large part of *eudaimonia* or human flourishing is "civic friendship." Contributing to the polis, notes Aristotle, primarily means when engaging in civic friendship, one understands and embodies that what is good for another is good for oneself, and what is good for oneself is good for the other. Aristotle concludes that the polis exists for human flourishing. Thus, according to Aristotelian ethics, being a "citizen of the polis" and belonging to the world is inherently connected to the social practices—e.g., music education and community music—where one learns and experiences various ways of being; belonging to the polis is, therefore, a potential means toward eudaimonia (Silverman & Elliott, 2016). Stated differently, the "tools" of social practices—e.g., music making of all kinds—are, like paideia, a means toward eudaimonia and the development of a flourishing personhood (Elliott & Silverman, 2015).

The Hull House

In the beginning, there were two women: Jane Addams (1860–1935) and Ellen Gates Starr (1859–1940). Both attended Rockford Female Seminary and over the years, Addams and Starr's relationship evolved and blossomed. In 1888, Addams and Starr—along with Sarah Anderson, another friend and Rockford Seminary teacher—travelled to Europe. Though the young women initially went abroad to appreciate and absorb art and culture, they also sought a sense of purpose for their lives.

This sense of purpose seemed clear upon visiting Toynbee Hall, a settlement house in one of London's disadvantaged neighborhoods. Operated by Oxford University graduates, wealthy young businessmen offered classes to their largely un-schooled neighbors. Toynbee Hall's charge was the social reformer, and religious cleric, Samuel Barnett (1898), who thought that settlements should provide a sense of relatedness and community (p. 11). He felt that, regardless of social strata, each person possessed the right to education, and, therefore, empowerment (Briggs & Macartney, 2013). For Barnett, everyone should have access to art, music, literature, and beyond; such exploration was not solely for the elite. Thus, he stated: "what is good enough for the University is good enough for East London." Despite his religious training, Barnett did not see his work as missionary (Briggs & Macartney, 2013; Siegel, 2012). Instead, Toynbee Hall's ethos was humanitarian (Briggs & Macartney, 2013). Many residents of the settlement not only continued their support of Toynbee Hall, but also continued a life of activism and service, such as Clement Attlee, Labor Party leader in 1935 and Prime Minister of the United Kingdom 1945–1951; and William Beveridge, British economist and Liberal politician, (Edmondson, 2013, p. 10)

The young American women were transformed by Barnett's work. Subsequently, in 1889, Addams and Starr (Berson, 2004) adopted some of Toynbee Hall's principles in the formation of the Hull House. As Addams (1899) notes, "the American Settlement, perhaps has not so much a sense of duty of the privileged toward the unprivileged, of the 'haves' to the 'have nots,'" but rather possesses "a desire to equalize" society and communities "through social effort … " (pp. 322–323). Addams and Starr sought support from local people and businesses, including from Helen Culver who inherited a "hospitable, old house" (Addams, 1910, p. 46) on Halstead Street in the 19th Ward from her cousin Charles Hull. Naming the settlement for the building's original owner, Addams and Starr rented and moved into Hull House in the midst of the working-class, immigrant neighborhood. Addams and Starr insisted "they must live among" the people "to learn first-hand the problems of their neighbors and to establish personal relationships with them" (Glowacki & Hendry, 2004, p. 7). During the earlier part of the twentieth century, living among those served departed radically from "established forms of philanthropy" (p. 7). For Addams and Starr, "settling" together with those they sought to help was not solely an effective way to assist those in need; also "it was a response" to what Addams perceived as the "polarizing effect of urban industrialization on American society" and to the various social, religious, and gendered inequities that threatened American democracy (p. 7).

Addams and Starr did not have a formal agenda for Hull House. They opened its doors and invited neighbors over. At first, Addams and Starr were the only "settlers" and organized activities for neighborhood children and adults. Within a month, and alongside Addams and Starr, volunteers such as Jennie Dow and Mary Rozet Smith began to systematize the educational offerings. Next, the women organized weekly receptions for adults, each one focusing on the ethnicities of participants "where food was served and participants were encouraged to chat, sing, and dance" (Streitmatter, 2012, p. 35). Eventually, this attracted large numbers to Hull House, which laid the foundation for a range of activities and academic courses.

The Hull House provided "a center for a higher civic and social life"; it sought "to institute and maintain educational and philanthropic enterprises, and to investigate and improve the conditions in the industrial districts of Chicago" (Addams, 1910, p. 89). The Hull House was not solely concerned with providing equal opportunities for residents and visitors, among other ethical considerations. Perhaps more importantly, both Addams and Starr wanted to get to know and learn from each person who happened to come to the Hull House. Consequently, their philanthropic work depended upon deeply understanding those they served.

Journalist Ida M. Tarbell stated in 1912: "Hull House is an 'open house' for its neighborhood. It is a place where men and women of all ages, conditions, and points of view are welcome ... Health, mind, morals, all are in its care" (quoted in Hamington, 2009, p. 3). Partially, this came to be because Hull House existed as a space where dialogue was fostered; it provided new immigrants ways to cope with the "modern city" and acted as a refuge for all who came into its doors (Glowacki & Hendry, 2004, p. 7) by creating an atmosphere of caring, compassion, dignity, respect, and understanding (Knight, 2008). Addams and Starr assisted those in need, caring for neighboring children, attending to those who were sick, and paying social visits to those who appeared lonely (p. 3).

As Louise Knight (2010) notes elsewhere, the Hull House sought to engage

> the human spirit ... its social clubs, classes and public lectures in the humanities and the arts, and music concerts—as well as the elegance of

> the building itself, [sought] to spark the imagination and feed the universal capacity for joy. [Addams's] interest in human fellowship arose out of the same passion.
>
> (p. 73)

Hull House expanded rapidly, both in size and scope, to include programs and living quarters across thirteen buildings. The first new expansion in 1890 was the Butler Gallery, Chicago's first public art gallery, which maintained not only the art gallery, but also a branch of the public library, and contained classrooms. As Starr noted: "the hungry individual soul which without art will have passed unsolaced and unfed, followed by other souls who lack the impulse his should have given" (cited in Addams, 1910, p. 159).[3] Soon afterward, in 1893, the Hull House Music School was established.

The Hull House Music School

The Hull House Music School was situated on the fourth floor of the Children's House (Hull House Association, 1907, p. 5). Even though the Hull House Music School served thousands of people across diverse age groups and cultural backgrounds by the 1920s, very little research investigates the historical and musical ramifications of this institution (notable exceptions: Elrod, 2001; Vaillant, 2003). In fact, Addams and Starr are not names that usually come to mind when considering the history of music education or community music in America. However, Addams, Starr, and Eleanor Smith[4] (who headed the Hull House Music School from 1893–1935) believed that music served an important place in education and could be powerful in social and emotional "reform," principles consistent with Aristotelian notions of eudaimonia. Thus, the Hull House Music School sought to provide creative, innovative programs for all, while simultaneously accepting responsibility for others by advocating for positive changes in public policy; it provided a model that enacted the quest for a "good life."

Moreover, Addams, Starr, Smith, and numerous other Hull House activists believed that music's potential to foster social cohesion, social wellbeing, and cultural exchange was as untapped as it was limitless. Because of this, musical outreach programs through the Hull House were plentiful. At the Hull House Music School, individuals could formally study music, attend a Sunday classical concert series, engage in men's, women's, and children's choruses; additionally, there were folk music experiences available for the social clubs and dancing activities at the settlement. Also, and perhaps more public, in 1907 the sixty-member Hull House Boys Band was established. Meeting all year long—unlike some of the other clubs and activities established at Hull House, the band rehearsed even during the summer months—the band gave concerts at both Hull House and a nearby country club;

additionally, "a contingent of the Hull-House Boys Band, with their band-master, went to the Front, and were afterwards taken into the occupied territory [to entertain the troops during World War I]" (Bryan & Davis, 1990, p. 163).[5] All was crafted to engender an invigorated sense of democratic, civic life where belonging was key to living in the urban environment.

By way of stressing music's potential toward transformation, Addams and Smith collaborated on the song, "A House Stands on a Busy Street." Addams wrote the song's lyrics while Smith wrote the music. It served the Hull House Women's Club, but can be seen as the "anthem" of the Hull House as a whole. Additionally, according to Derek Vaillant (2003), this song epitomizes the important place music had for the settlement:

> Some hours they sit 'neath music's spell
> And when the air is rife,
> With all the magic of sweet sound
> It heals the pang of life …

Here, music helped give the immigrants and diverse laborers who visited Hull House a means of escape and solace. However, this musical escape not only provided the means to dream through "sweet sound"; it promoted important social possibility. Thus, the verse continues with:

> Some hours they dream of civic pride
> Of cities that shall be,
> Within whose streets each citizen,
> Shall live life worthily.

As Vaillant (2003) argues, this song—along with numerous songs choral director and composer Eleanor Smith wrote for the Hull House and its people—spoke to the daily lives of those engaged with "A House on a Busy Street." In fact, most of Smith's compositions were "mirrors" for the people of Hull House. Her songs engage with themes and topics such as women's suffrage, needing improved labor conditions, and respect for workers and laborers (Elrod, 2001). "A House Stands on a Busy Street" also stood for progressive values: fostering equality and equity amongst people (women's rights, establishing child labor laws, establishing labor union); social association and communal engagement/responsibility; and more. These values denoted the philosophical principles of the Hull House and the Hull House Music School, and affected the constituency of those who crossed through its doors.

Hull House leaders thought "that wider access to high-quality music education" could and would improve the lives of working-class Chicagoans (Vaillant, 2003). And while Starr was passionate about art and music, she deferred to Addams when it came to the Hull House Music School. Because of this, Addams and Smith developed most of the programming and curriculum for the Hull House Music School.

Addams and Smith were not always in agreement of "what" and "whose" music would count as "high-quality" music education. Should the Hull House Music School focus on "popular, accessible" music, or should reformers challenge audiences' musical experiences with the risk of alienating diverse peoples? Smith defended the importance of classical repertoire and "advocated presenting challenging programs as a worthy reform end in itself" (Vaillant, p. 102). Addams did not agree. She felt that music should be a uniting force, and a recruitment tool to promote the Hull House and its aims. Compromise was reached: they frequently programmed classical compositions such as arias from Mozart operas juxtaposed with marches, waltzes, and familiar songs. It is worth noting that this argument took place in 1898. The music education community and its practitioners, as well as some within the field of community music, are still debating the importance of this very issue (e.g., Powell & Smith, 2019).

While Addams believed that the school should "give a thorough musical instruction to a limited number of children" (meaning the talented, but disenfranchised), she felt this was a great need; a number of Chicago musical centers already served those who could afford it. Regarding the Hull House Music School, Addams (1910) said: "from their first lessons they are taught to compose…the school is able to recover the songs of the immigrants through the children. Some of these folk songs have never been committed to paper … " (p. 163). Fees for ten lessons (in 1900) cost $1, though many students were taught for free since they could not afford this. Addams (1910) explains: "we constantly see the most promising musical ability extinguished when the young people enter industries which so sap their vitality that they cannot carry on serious study in the scanty hours outside of the factory work" (p. 163).

Vaillant notes:

> By acknowledging music's power to transform identity and civic life, musical progressivism at Hull House brought together a diverse community of individuals who found expression, social contact and a variety of resources with which to explore the interplay of art and civic engagement … Despite the occasional patronizing commentary, and despite the seeming contradiction between the aim of overcoming "differences" and the goal of strategically "preserving" musical heritage, musical outreach at Hull House did not suppress or obliterate cultural differences. Those differences were multiplied, instead, and with them the democratic possibilities of urban public culture increased as well.
>
> (p. 124).

The musical ends of the Hull House Music School were intimately connected to the ends of communal living and democratic ways of being. Such living and being are at the heart of any understanding of eudaimonia.

John Dewey (1930) states:

> In these days of criticism of democracy as a political institution, Miss Addams has reminded us that democracy is … a way of living together and working together. I doubt if any other one agency can be found which has touched so many people and brought to them a conception of the real meaning of the spirit of the common life.
>
> (quoted in Longo, 2012, p. 45)

Addams's thoughts and deeds not only fueled the philosophy and practices of Dewey's Chicago Laboratory School[6] (Leffers, 1993; Seigfried, 1999; Silverman, 2012); they presaged the contributions of many of today's most esteemed socio-political feminist theorists and care ethicists (Anderson, 2004; Hamington, 2001).

The Hull House, Eudaimonia, and an Ethic of Care

Despite early efforts to "do good," Addams and Starr knew that to make an impact on those at Hull House, they would need the financial and practical support of upper-class young women. One such volunteer was the previously mentioned Mary Rozet Smith, Addams's life-long partner. Aiming to keep the young men off the streets, Smith bought pool tables and chess sets; she read aloud to the boys and began teaching kindergarten and music classes (Streitmatter, 2012). She also helped in all aspects of Hull House's theater productions. Beyond this, Smith provided Addams and Starr with the necessary funding to expand their offerings and programs. Smith's money built a children's playground, bought an organ to support the music program, and expanded construction for a new building for children's activities.

Addams and Starr recruited the assistance of other wealthy women to provide funding and services to Hull House insofar as it went from a single building to several, including a gymnasium and a residence hall for adult men. Because of this, Hull House yielded a communal living space "that allowed independence but also the support and companionship of like-minded people." At a time and place where "women's roles were severely restricted," the Hull House provided women the opportunity "to emerge into public life as leaders, teachers, social investigators, activists, and organizers" (Glowacki & Hendry, 2004, p. 8).

Relatedly, Hull House possessed a "nurturing" presence. In the beginning, Hull House was "a community of university women" intent upon creating and sustaining social and educational opportunities for working-class people (especially European immigrants) in the surrounding Chicago neighborhood. Hull House was, and became known as, a place and space based on and motivated by an ethic of community, concern, relief, and socio-political activism for people in need (Hamington, 2009). Thus, Hull House and the work of these university women was a working site of *eudaimonia.*

The interconnectedness and communal eudaimonic sensibilities of the Hull House were intended "to provide a center for a higher civic and social life; to institute and maintain educational and philanthropic enterprises, and to investigate and improve the conditions in the industrial districts of Chicago" (Addams, 1910/1981, p. 89). Flexibility, tolerance, hospitality, a readiness to experiment, sympathy, and community mindedness were the kinds of dispositions Addams believed must be present in Hull House residents. And all activity of the Hull House was grounded in:

> the solidarity of the human race … [its residents] must be content to live quietly side by side with their neighbors, until they grow into a sense of relationship and mutual interests … They are bound to see the needs of their neighborhood as a whole … They are bound to regard the entire life of their city as organic, to make an effort to unify it, and to protest against its overdifferentiation.
>
> (Addams, 1910/1981, pp. 98–100)

It seems clear that these are the issues inherent in an ethic of care, one that places emphasis on "personal connection, context, and affective responses" (Hamington, 2001, p. 107). Addams assumed a universalized caring standpoint, one that begins with the ethos of communal living.[7]

For Addams, an ethical way of being maintains an interconnectedness of and, therefore, respect for self-and-other: "This respect requires us to take responsive action to the perceived needs of self, other individuals, and communities" (Leffers, 1993, p. 73). Indeed, no person is an island, and self-other, neighborhood, community are connected in Addams's mind. This ethos asks us to consider the "whole" person and a person's whole humanity: body, mind, emotions, spirituality, needs, volitions, memories, identities, talents, and abilities. For Addams, this "whole" mattered; at Hull House people were appreciated and educated to have an informed, empathetic voice (Leffers, 1993). Addams believed when "difference"—whether difference of opinion, experience, worldview—rises to the level of consciousness, people should cherish that difference and work together to appreciate it. The broader community under Addams's guidance asks us to value the individual as connected to the community and its greater good. So, Addams's Hull House and the beliefs this settlement "embodied" asks its people to refine and redefine the ongoing experiment that is an American democracy.

Philosophers of education often connect the work of Addams and Dewey. And rightly so; they had a close friendship and were good colleagues. Addams invited Dewey to speak at Hull House on numerous occasions; Addams lectured in Dewey's classes at the University of Chicago. However, many scholars position Addams in deference to Dewey, when this is inaccurate. In fact, much of Dewey's philosophy is indebted to Addams and the Hull House, for "Addams and Dewey were intellectual soul mates from the moment they met in 1892" (Hamington, 2009, p. 37). As Dewey admits: "I cannot tell you how much good I got from my stay at Hull House. My indebtedness to you for giving me an insight into matters there is great" (quoted in Daynes & Longo, 2004, p. 7). Notably, "Dewey dedicated *Liberalism and Social Action* to Addams and named one of his daughters in her honor" (Hamington, 2009, p. 37). Additionally, Seigfried (1999) notes that Dewey's (1916) *Democracy and education* is largely based upon his experiences at Hull House (p. 213).

Still, Dewey is known as the great intellectual philosopher or thinker and Addams as the woman activist or doer. As Maurice Hamington (2009) posits, Dewey and Addams "are perceived as classic stereotypes of gender: the male as mind generating theory, and the woman as body experiencing and caring. However, there is much evidence that this characterization is inaccurate" (p. 37). Hamington (2009) concludes: "Perhaps one of the factors in the historical oversight of Addams's impact on Dewey is the lack of direct references to Addams in Dewey's writing. Writers of the era were less meticulous about attribution than they are today" (p. 38). Still, one thing is clear: they both benefitted from each other in numerous ways.

Like Addams, Dewey believed that life was not something that happened to us, but something we enact. In much of his writing, Dewey notes of the connectivity of human experience and understanding (Shusterman, 2000), primarily because everything we engage with, we do so "from a personal standpoint—our projects are imbued with all of our hopes, fears, expectations, values, and limitations, whether they are claimed to be purely intellectual activities or not" (Leffers, 1993, p. 70). Dewey underscores this approach in most topics he investigates, including understanding the natures of education, the arts, and more. In *Pragmatist Aesthetics*, Richard Shusterman (2000) emphasizes that Dewey sought to integrate life, art, and experience as well as to democratize the arts in the sense of putting the arts to work for the betterment of society. Jane Addams's Hull House epitomized this belief in reality.

The work of Addams and Dewey—both in theory and practice—helps remind us of the connectedness of self and other. Reminded of this, we should live a life of meaningfulness and significance; empathetically connected to others and the world around us. Once we see and understand ourselves as connected and (hopefully) "globalized," then problems for our friends, neighbors, and the world at large are problems for us (e.g., Sevenhuijsen, 1998;

Tronto, 1995). We must do our best to find solutions to problems; we must take action and help those we can. So, in line with some of Aristotle's thinking, we must be concerned with civic friendship as it pertains to the polis, thus potentially achieving a sense of eudaimonia for oneself and the worlds around us.

Implications

Where and why music making and music teaching and learning occur directly impact the values of the musical engagements and experiences (Elliott & Silverman, 2015). The case of the Hull House provides implications for the here and now, because of the degrees and levels of communal living with musical engagements. In terms of music making and music teaching and learning—of all kinds and in all spaces—music is "good for" many things, too numerous to mention. Because of the positive musical-emotional experiences music listening and music making potentially arouse and express, music—taught educatively and ethically—can make major differences in peoples' lives (e.g., Elliott & Silverman, 2015). When music making and music teaching and learning are ethically guided—when we engage people not only in and about music but also *through* music—we have greater opportunities to strive for and achieve many dimensions of eudaimonia. The challenge, then, is to help musicians of all kinds, including music educators and community music facilitators, to become more aware of all that eudaimonia involves and that is available and achievable through educative and ethical music making and music teaching and learning. Sites such as the Hull House are reminders that this kind of good work has been accomplished in meaningful ways.

Through looking at past models—and researching current models—of eudaimonia for music teaching and learning, music educators and community music facilitators can examine ways to teach connection and care; music educators in positions of teacher education can find ways to teach teachers to teach connection and care; music education scholars can further research connection and care and publish more on such important issues such as these. Beyond this, we all can strive to maintain and expand our awareness of our interconnection with others. We should recognize our dependence on others and that this dependence does not make us weaker, but stronger. Or, to use the words of Jane Addams (1910), we should "exchange for the music of isolated voices the volume and strength of the chorus" (p. 60).

Notes

1. In 1915, Addams became Chair of the Women's Peace Party; that same year, she became President of the International Congress of Women. Later, Addams served as President of the Women's International League for Peace and Freedom until 1929.

As stated by the Nobel Organization: "After sustaining a heart attack in 1926, Miss Addams never fully regained her health. Indeed, she was being admitted to a Baltimore hospital on the very day, December 10, 1931, that the Nobel Peace Prize was being awarded to her in Oslo. She died in 1935 three days after an operation revealed unsuspected cancer. The funeral service was held in the courtyard of Hull-House" (see www.nobelprize.org/prizes/peace/1931/addams/biographical/).

2. It is beyond the scope of this chapter to explore class and race issues found at the Hull House. For such examinations, see Thomas Lee Philpott (1991), Rivka Shpak Lissak (1989), Gwendolyn Mink (1995), amongst others. As Eleanor Stebner (1997) illustrates, "issues of race and class" should be acknowledged; however, "it is inappropriate to apply late-twentieth-century standards to nineteenth-century persons" (p. 25).
3. Notable and important firsts, Hull House saw to establishing the first citizenship preparation classes in the United States, first community theater in the United States, and, among other things, established the city's first public playground and first free art exhibits.
4. Eleanor Smith previously worked at the Francis Parker Normal School in Chicago and helped create music reforms in teacher training at the University of Chicago's Education Department, then run by John Dewey.
5. A more well-known member of this, then, all-boys band was clarinetist, Benny Goodman. Other notable Hull House alumni: Art Hodes, Milt Hinton, and James C. Petrillo (trumpet player who organized the American Federation of Musicians).
6. The Chicago Laboratory School, founded in 1896 by Dewey, meant to be a site to test-out progressive ideals of education in an actual school setting.
7. For example, one action item was that of garbage collection. The sheer number of large refuse piles, dead animals that did not get taken care of, as well as the debris from the tenements and stables that weren't connected to Chicago's sewer system; all of this caused the neighborhood to have an extremely high death rate. By working together, neighbors and residents helped to implement changes needed in the city's refuse-collection system, which in turn improved their own living conditions. This is just one example of the kind of communalism that existed as the foundation for the Hull House.

References

Addams, J. (1899). A function of the social settlement. Reprinted in Christopher Lasch, Ed. *The Social Thought of Jane Addams*. Indianapolis, IN: The Bobbs-Merrill Company, Inc., 1965.

Addams, J. (1910). *Twenty years at Hull House*. New York: New American Library.

Allsup, R. E., & Shieh, E. (2012). Social justice and music education. *Music Educators Journal. 98*(4), 47–51.

Anderson, M. E. (2004). Jane Addams' democracy and social ethics: Defending care ethics, *Macalester Journal of Philosophy. 13*(1), http://digitalcommons.macalester.edu/philo/vol. 13/iss1/2

Barnett, S. A. (1898) University settlements. In W. Reason (Ed.) *University and social Settlements*. London: Methuen.

Berson, R. K. (2004). *Jane Addams: A biography*. Westport, CN: Greenwood Press.

Briggs, A., & Macartney, A. (2013). *Toynbee Hall (Routledge Revivals): The first hundred years*. New York: Routledge.

Bryan, M. L., & Davis, A. F., (Ed.). (1990). *One hundred years at Hull House*. Bloomington, IN: Indiana University Press.

Crittenden, J., & Levine, P. (2013). Civic education, *The Stanford Encyclopedia of Philosophy,* E. N. Zalta (Ed.), http://plato.stanford.edu/archives/sum2013/entries/civic-education/

Daynes, G., & Longo, N. (2004). Jane Addams and the origins of service-practice in the United States. *Michigan Journal of Community Service Learning. 11*(1), 5–13.

Edmondson, D. (2013). *Social work practice theory.* London: Sage.

Elliott, D. J., & Silverman, M. (2015). *Music matters: A philosophy of music education.* New York: Oxford University Press.

Elrod, P. G. (2001). Vocal music at the Hull House, 1889–1942: An overview of choral and singing class events and a study of the life and works of Eleanor Smith, founder of the Hull House Music School. Dissertation, University of Illinois, Urbana.

Fotopoulos, T. (2003). From (mis)education to *Paideia. Democracy and Nature. 2*(1), 15–50.

Glowacki, P., & Hendry, J. (2004). *Images of Hull-House*. Charleston, SC: Arcadia Publishing.

Hamington, M. (2001). Jane Addams and the politics of embodied care, *Journal of Speculative Philosophy. 15*(2), 105–121.

Hamington, M. (2009). *The social philosophy of Jane Addams.* Urbana, IL: University of Illinois Press.

Held, V. (2006). *The ethics of care: Personal, political, and global*. New York: Oxford University Press.

Hoagland, S. L. (1991). Some thought about caring. In C. Card (Ed.), *Feminist ethics* (pp. 246–263). Lawrence, KS: University Press of Kansas.

Howe, S. W. (2014). *Women music educators in the United States: A history.* Lanham, MD: Scarecrow Press.

Hull House Association. (1907). *Hull House bulletin.* vol 5–7, Chicago, IL.

Jaggar, J. M. (1995). Caring as a feminist practice of moral reasoning. In V. Held (Ed.), *Justice and care: Essential readings in feminist ethics* (pp. 179–202). Boulder, CO: Westview Press.

Kittay Feder, E., & D. Meyers, (Eds.) (1987). *Women and moral theory*. Lanham, MD: Rowman & Littlefield.

Knight, L. (2008). *Citizen Jane Addams and the struggle for democracy*. Chicago, IL: University of Chicago Press.

Knight, L. (2010). *Jane Addams: Spirit in action.* New York: W. W. Norton & Company.

Laird, S. (2009). Musical hunger: A philosophical testimonial of miseducation. *Philosophy of Music Education Review. 17*(1), 4–21.

Leffers, M. R. (1993). Pragmatists Jane Addams and John Dewey inform the ethic of care. *Hypatia. 8*(2), 64–77.

Leglar, M. A., & Smith, D. S. (2010). Community music in the United States: An overview of origins and evolution. *The International Journal of Community Music. 10*(3), 343–353.

Lissak, R. S. (1989). *Pluralism and progressives: Hull House and the new immigrants, 1890–1919*. Chicago, IL: The University of Chicago Press.

Longo, N. V. (2012). *Why community matters: Connecting education with civic life.* Albany, NY: State University of New York Press.

Mink, G. (1995). *The wages of motherhood: Inequality in the welfare state, 1917–1942.* Ithaca, NY: Cornell University Press.

Murray, P., & Wilson, P. (Eds.). (2004). *Music and the muses: The culture of mousike in the classical Athenian city.* New York: Oxford University Press.

Noddings, N. (2003). *Caring: A feminine approach to ethics and moral education.* Berkeley, CA: University of California Press.

Noddings, N. (2010). *The maternal factor: Two paths to morality.* Berkeley, CA: University of California Press.

Orr, D. W. (2004). *Earth in mind: On education, environment, and the human prospect.* London: Island Press.

Philpott, T. L. (1991). *The slum and the ghetto: Immigrants, blacks, and reformers in Chicago, 1880–1930.* Belmont, CA: Wadsworth Publishing Company.

Powell, B., & Smith, G. D. (2019). Philosophy of assessment in popular music education. In D.J. Elliott, M. Silverman, & G. McPherson (Eds.), *The Oxford handbook of philosophical and qualitative assessment in music education* (pp. 347–364). New York: Oxford University Press.

Seigfried, C. H. (1999). Socializing democracy: Jane Addams and John Dewey. *Philosophy of the Social Sciences. 29*(2), 207–230.

Sevenhuijsen, S. (1998). *Citizenship and the ethics of care: Feminist considerations on justice, morality, and politics.* New York: Routledge.

Shusterman, R. (2000). *Pragmatist aesthetics: Living beauty, rethinking art* (2nd ed.). Lanham, MD: Rowman & Littlefield Education.

Siegel, D. (2012). *Charity and condescension: Victorian literature and the dilemmas of philanthropy.* Athens, OH: Ohio University Press.

Silverman, M. (2012). John Dewey and James Mursell: An introduction. *Visions of Research in Music Education, 21.* Retrieved from www.rider.edu/~vrme

Silverman, M., & Elliott, D. J. (2016). Arts education as/for artistic citizenship. In D. J. Elliott, M. Silverman, & W. Bowman (Eds.), *Artistic citizenship: Artistry, social responsibility, and ethical praxis* (pp. 81–103). New York: Oxford University Press.

Stebner, E. (1997). *The women of Hull House: A study in spirituality, vocation, and friendship.* Albany, NY: State University of New York Press.

Slote, M. (2007). *The ethics of care and empathy.* New York: Routledge.

Streitmatter, R. (2012). *Outlaw marriages: The hidden histories of fifteen extraordinary same-sex couples.* Boston, MA: Beacon Press.

Tronto, J. (1995). Care as a basis for radical political judgements. *Hypatia. 10*(2), 141–49.

Vaillant, D. (2003). *Sounds of reform: Progressivism & music in Chicago, 1873–1935.* Chapell Hill, NC: The University of North Carolina Press.

Vogel, D. (2013). "To put beauty into the world": Music education resources in The Ladies' Home Journal, 1890–1919. *Journal of Historical Research in Music Education.* XXXIV(2), 119–136.

Volk, T. M. (1998). *Music, education, and multiculturalism: Foundations and principles.* New York: Oxford University Press.

Wright, F.A. (1969/1923). *The arts in Greece; three essays.* Port Washington, NY: Kennikat Press.

4 The Happy Basket

Kathleen Dean Moore

Is that what you really want, or did nobody ask you?

Libby Roderick

I embarked on an experiment this year. On January 1, I put a basket on my desk, and every time I found myself really happy—happy in that deep-down, exhaling, head-back way—I jotted down on a little slip of paper what I was doing at that time and threw the paper into the basket. My plan was that at the end of the year (I pictured myself home alone, maybe on a cloudy, winter day with the lamps on and the furnace sighing), I would spread the papers across the dining room table and study them. I imagined what that would be, to read them all, remembering. I would arrange them in piles by whatever categories suggested themselves—time, place, companions, activity, degrees of temperature, sobriety, or sunlight. This would be important data.

So many people are telling me what should make me happy. Buy a cute new car. Be thin. Get promoted or honored or given a raise. Travel: Baja! Belize! Finish the laundry. The voices may or may not be my own; they are so insistent that I can't distinguish them from the ringing in my ears. Maybe they are the voices of my mother and father, long dead and well-intended, wanting only that I would be happy. Or my husband Frank, fully alive but ditto in all other respects. My colleagues. Maybe they're the voices of advertisers, popular song-writers, even the president. Most of the time, I don't even think about making choices, plowing through my life as if I were pulled by a mule.

I wanted to think about this for myself. I wanted to spend some time—no, not *spend.* I wanted to create some time to think about happiness on a quiet winter day, with data. I thought that if I could see the haphazard heaps of happiness, I could come to understand something about what I should do. Be glad and grateful, for one thing. Absolutely. But more than that: If I knew what made me really happy, I could leave behind the false starts and destructive agendas and organize my life a better way. I could lead an intentional life. I could resist being distracted by people who would sell me happiness, or give it to me in tiny pellets when I pushed whatever lever they thought needed pushing. It would be time well spent, I thought, shuffling these moments in my hands, lining them up on the table.

The first decision was about the basket itself, the shape and substance of it. I considered a basket my son Jonathan had made of tule reeds, a sway-backed arrangement woven of his love for damp places that smell of fish. But it would prejudice my experiment, I decided, to use this basket. I considered the tea box my daughter Erin made for me of balsawood beautifully fitted and painted yellow. "May you find peace and contentment at the bottom of your cup," the lid says and so I dismissed this possibility too. I wanted the result of my experiment to be a surprise. I settled on a pink Easter basket, picked out the last shreds of plastic grass, and put it on my desk.

I thought it was worth a try for a year.

So here I am, eight months later, four months before the experiment is to end, hugely tempted to take a peek at the early data. I think this might bias the results, like opening the oven door to take a look at the soufflé. There's an intriguing pile inside the basket, scraps of paper and folded sheets of computer-printed prose, post-it notes. Maybe I should just pull the papers out and straighten them. I bet lots of scientists peek at their results before the experiment's over, and I want to read my happiness—it's been kind of a worthless day.

Walked out to the bridge early in the morning. Kestrel in the maple, cow parsnips beginning to bloom. Every person I passed said, "Morning." Not "good morning." Just "Morning!" It didn't have to be good. It was enough that it was morning. Morning! An army guy running. Morning! The lady with the cocker spaniel. Morning! A young man jogging. Morning, morning, morning, three white-haired women. Morning, morning, morning, I said back.

* * *

Went with Frank to a program on Lou Gehrig's disease. Allen was there, in a wheelchair. A woman explained that, as time went on, he would lose the power to speak, eventually able to move only his eyes. To help him communicate, they would post three columns of the things he would most likely want to say. If he wanted to say, "I love you," for example, he could move his eyes to indicate A17. The woman said that of all the things that Lou Gehrig's disease brings, the most striking is the outpouring of love. At that, Allen started to sob. The woman explained that too, telling us that people who lose control of their muscles will cry often. "Think of how much muscle it takes to keep your crying inside you, every muscle tensed to hold in your sorrow," she said. I had never thought of that. People pulled their chairs closer to Allen, and his friend stroked his back, and there wasn't anybody muscular enough to hold in their sadness, and that was important and good.

* * *

On a morning walk. The College of Agriculture cows all have bright day-glow orange spots on their rumps, as if they sat in the paint pot. The indignity makes me laugh. But the sound of the cows ripping grass with their flat teeth —this reassures me, and seems to be all the cows care about.

* * *

Went to hear the Ode to Joy, *Beethoven's Ninth, Marlan conducting. Went alone, Frank in Denver. Couldn't keep myself from thinking what I would write for the happy basket, which made me feel like a cheater. But when the chorus kicked in at the end, and the trumpets started to sing, Marlan leaning in, wiping sweat off his forehead with the back of his tuxedo cuff without dropping the baton or pausing, and the music marching up and down again, and the sopranos impossibly ... what ... impossibly high and clear and triumphant, all I could think was what a glory, what a glory. If humans can do this, can do this TOGETHER, then they can do anything. You know that point in the* Ode to Joy *when you think there will be a rest and there ISN'T?—it's about going on and not stopping. Thrilled by the music, thrilled by the hope, the conviction that if we can go on, can just hold on long enough to get past this point in history, just keep playing the* Ode to Joy, *just hold things together through this time, then maybe there is hope for the human race. If we can't, then the world can go on without us, but that would be a shame, because it would have to go on without the* Ode to Joy.

* * *

Rain, after no rain. And company for dinner, after a long time without seeing friends.

* * *

Phone message from Erin. Nothing to say, really, but she sounded content. She had had a good day. I could tell by her voice she was healthy. This makes a mother glad.

* * *

We were all piled into the drift boat on the Rogue River, Frank and I in the bow, Jon on the oars, Erin in the stern. It'd been a gentle river, clear blue-grey, braiding between gravel bars and huge slash piles of flood-torn trees. Then suddenly we were between bedrock boulders. The river picked up speed, falling quickly over a series of shelves, through a boulder field. Frank and I leveled our weight and hung on; there wasn't time for life jackets. Jon pointed the bow into the current and hauled back on the oars, slipping the boat around each boulder in turn, averting catastrophe after catastrophe, dropping into standing waves that threw up the bow and splashed it down again and spit us out at the bottom of the drop. I could feel Jon's strength—my grown son on the oars—and Frank's relief—the father, trusting. In the stern, Erin whooped and pounded Jon on the head. From then on, we floated through gentle water and thin sun. There was a great blue heron and a good view of the mountains between clouds.

* * *

Class went well today. Students prepared and excited. After class, a student said thank you. It's a heady experience to have a class go well. A class is kind of a garage band, everybody pounding away on their own instruments, and something new and interesting and celebratory flying into the air.

* * *

Something my student told me: That in southwestern deserts there is a giant water bug that can tell in advance when a flash flood is coming and run for the hills. This made me happy and hopeful. If giant bugs can sense impending disaster and change their behavior to avoid it, is this something human beings might also be able to do?

* * *

I'm lying on my back under ponderosa trees by Davis Lake. The layer of silky pine needles must be a foot thick, and warm. And sweet. I had gone out to look for birds, but this is better, letting them come to me. Chickadees. Juncos. Yellow-rumped warblers. Nuthatches. I can hear the lake lap in the tule reeds. I smell water and ashes. Davis Lake burned last summer, a horrific forest fire that burned for two weeks. But this patch of ponderosas was spared. I'm happy there are birds.

* * *

Frank and I held hands in bed last night, as we often do. We lay on our backs and held hands. This makes me happy, feeling the warmth and strength of him beside me.

* * *

Fresh crab.

* * *

Dreamed about Jonathan last night. He was young, maybe four or five years old, and he was sitting on this little chair. Erin was there too, and lots of other people. He might have been on a platform of some kind, maybe a stage, because our heads were all about the same height. He said, "Mom." I was talking to somebody and didn't turn to him—you know, like parents and little kids. So he said it again: "MOM." I kept on talking. He said, "MOM!" and I turned to him. He didn't say anything, but he got up out of the little chair and walked over and wrapped his arms around my neck in a big hug. I held him too, for the longest time, and even though it was just a dream, it was one of the most satisfying and peaceful moments of my life.

And now that I write this, I am wondering if it was a dream, or if it's a memory.

* * *

Got called back for a second mammogram. A common thing; shouldn't worry. But I did, of course, imagining a black river spreading like a delta over my heart. My breasts prickled and kept me awake. Then, a week later: all okay. Frank doesn't rejoice with me; if he was happy now, he would have to admit he was worried then.

* * *

Walking up over a rise in the sand dunes. Red patches on blackbirds' shoulders, like the flames kids paint on their pickups. I have never seen them so extravagant. At the top of the rise, a blaze of reflected light and the salty, stinging smell of the sea. If I could mainline that smell, I could live like an ecstatic.

* * *

Walking fast in the morning, down the path to the bridge.

* * *

A patch of sun and a glass of wine after work.

* * *

Tired, and a load of firewood stacked in the garage. It's oak and maple that Frank and I cut at the farm: Frank cutting wood in a cloud of noise and fumes, emerging from the smoke covered with woodchips. Me darting in to pick up the logs and chuck them toward the van. Then picking them up again and rubbing off thick layers of moss and lichen, liverwort and licorice fern. The smell is so sweet, so damp and deep forest. Then splitting the wood in the driveway, the solid chunk and wood laying itself down in neat halves.

Would it be cheating to make some preliminary observations?

I'm surprised at how often ideas make me happy: a new point of view, an analogy. Movement shows up a lot—walking, especially. Contact with my grown children, no matter how tenuous—a phone call, a memory. Contact with the renewing, natural world, often through smell or sound: this is big. Music. Change from routine, or relief after a challenge. Almost all the happy moments take place in a pause, a slowing down from job and routine: this is probably an important observation. I'm surprised how many of these pleasures are solitary, and I wonder if this is my nature or my choice, or an artifact of the experimental design. In my notes, there's an odd relationship between happiness and sadness, which makes me wonder if these are opposing emotions after all, or if the opposite of happiness might be something else—meaninglessness, maybe, or emptiness. I'm sort of surprised that for eight months, there aren't more happy moments, and I wonder if I'm living my life like a flat brain wave, or if I'm just unreliable about taking notes. I don't know what a normal allotment of happiness is, I guess.

When I compare the happy basket to my calendar, I see that there is little meaningful relationship between what I put on my calendar and what I put in the happy basket. I'm reminded of all the time-heavy things that don't show up in the stack of papers. There's no mention of my promotion—*la de da*. No mention of ticking things off a to-do list. No competition for reputation, the human motivation that causes Hobbes so much trouble and takes so much time and attention. There's no mention of shopping or possessing, although adequate income is a baseline firmly and invisibly supporting each entry. There's really no explicit mention of helping other people. Technology is invisibly present in the phone calls and automobiles and in a few cases, airplanes, that support these experiences, but in nowhere near the quantities proportional to the time I sink into it. Good health lurks in every entry. As for my calling, teaching shows up, but writing doesn't, and of the trappings of writing—the acceptances and invitations and kind letters—nary a one.

I'm warning myself against generalizing from my own experience, but of course that's what I'm going to do. So, okay: I would suggest that the elements of happiness might include (1) a certain baseline standard of security; (2) significant contact with the natural world, its sights and smells and sounds and comfort; (3) meaningful work; (4) family or some other set of people who love you and whom you deeply love; (5) stimulating ideas; (6) celebratory arts—and (7) the time to pause to notice these and rejoice in them.

Walking on the headland, we found the impression where an animal had slept in a bed of iris. Mist so thick we had to take the presence of the ocean on faith.

*

New-dug radishes from Denison Farm.

5 Musicophilia, Biophilia, and the Human Prospect

David W. Orr

The warnings from scientists could not be clearer: the time to act to avoid climate catastrophe and preserve a habitable Earth is very short (McKibben, 2018; Mora et al., 2018; U.S. Global Change Research Program, 2018). The forces unraveling the Creation are a juggernaut eliminating species and entire ecosystems (Kolbert, 2014). Ahead, looms the prospect of "cascading system failures threatening basic necessities like food supply and electricity" (Damasio, 2018, pp. 216–217), and ungovernable societies (Sengupta, 2018; Steffen et al., 2018). None of this is new. For many years, scientists have been warning us that we were on course to irretrievably mutilate Earth and jeopardize our collective future (Union of Concerned Scientists, 1992). Still, we dawdle. Appeals to our rationality, morality, concern for our progeny, and even to our self-interest have not moved us to do nearly enough to avert the destruction of civilization. From their perch in the commanding corporate heights the best and brightest argue that preventative action is warranted only if it generates a profit. Merely saving the world is well, oh so quaint.

Our common predicament has been central to my life and career as a teacher, writer, and organizer (Orr, 1992, 2004, 2010, 2016). Our failure to act commensurate with the scale, duration, and salience of the multiple threats to our common future leads me to ask about other ways to motivate action while there is still time. However important data, science, logic, and reason certainly are, they have not moved enough of us, enough of the time to do nearly enough.

This essay is a speculation about the power of music to help do what rationality alone and appeals to profit have failed to do. I wonder about the possibility of using music to unite the two hemispheres of mind that divide rationality from emotion and detachment from engagement and harness that more unified mind to a more impassioned and capable defense of life (McGilchrist, 2009; Midgley, 2010). I hasten to add that I have no musical qualifications whatsoever and none as a neuroscientist. For that reason among others, I conclude with lots of questions, not a "to do list" or a blueprint for action. I begin with a recollection from my admittedly nonmusical early life.

1

When my family would gather at Thanksgiving to express gratitude for their various blessings, the kids were required to display the results of our hours spent practicing the piano. My sister would quite properly play a piece of mid-level difficulty, receiving polite applause. I, in turn, would play a less difficult piece and the assembled would say things like "I didn't know a piano could make that kind of noise." My brother with even less aptitude but more determination would bang out some piece or other with brute force. My aunts, uncles, and cousins would stare at their shoes and mutter something to the effect that "well, it was better than last year." The finale always was my slightly older cousin, a concert pianist in her early teens, playing something she'd just performed with some symphony orchestra or other, to rave reviews. The family showered her with rapturous praise. Alas, I knew then that I was not destined for a career in music and free to pursue other options.

In the years since, however, I have come to think that the ability to perform music at a high level is one thing, limited to those with talent, determination, and the 10,000 hours of practice said to be necessary to develop professional-grade skill in any endeavor. But the rest of us have, to one degree or another, an inborn affinity for music. For example, I wake up almost every morning with some tune, hymn, or random melody in my head. I whistle when I work around the yard or doing house chores. I can anticipate the next tune up on my hundreds of tapes of country music that I recorded three decades ago. Before any tape plays, I could not have recalled the sequence of tunes, but my brain somehow recorded it beneath my conscious thought so just before one song ends, I know what's coming next. Oliver Sacks (2007) calls this "a defenseless engraving of music on the brain … that may even occur in relatively unmusical people" (p. 47).

I like country music—the older kind that deals with pain, failure, suffering, and rainy nights. Songs like "Long Black Veil" transport me to some other place and time.[1] "Amazing Grace," or the "Ashokan Farewell" can move me to tears, but so can Elvis singing "Without Love" or the Righteous Brothers' "Unchained Melody." I can listen for hours to authentic country or blues, but can barely sit still for an hour in a concert of classical music for which I have "no ear" and even less patience. But I know that classical music in the background helps to pass the hours of long-distance driving and calm anxiety and road rage.

With or without musical ability, we are surrounded by and infused with music, and not all of it is made by humans. Birdsong, for example, fascinates me and I wonder whether birds sing for joy, to compete for mates, to defend their territory, or all of these. To that question, philosopher and musician, David Rothenberg (2005), believes that "there are no answers … just further dreams and guesses as to the elusive reasons why" (p. 218). I do not bother myself with such arcana but amuse myself sometimes by imitating a few bird songs like those of cardinals and chickadees in my backyard. Sometimes they reciprocate, until the particular bird with which I am conversing discovers that I have nothing important to say, or was saying it with the wrong accent, or was an imposter—an errant human trying to establish a cross-species relationship. It goes both ways, however. I once attended an open-air concert by the Paul Winter Consort, during which nearby whip-poor-wills enthusiastically joined in to the music. The audience gave them a rousing ovation and got a birdly encore in return.

Bug music is different (Rothenberg, 2013). When cicadas emerged from their 17-year slumber two summers ago, their constant noise enveloped our neighborhood like the roar of a machine. Cicadas have to mate quickly and are rather indiscriminate with who or what. One tried in vain to mate with my lawn tractor that was the right shade of red; another tried me. After several weeks they went back underground but will return in 2033 for another concert. How they detect the passage of time with such precision is yet another mystery.

The coyote packs that roamed the Ozark hills where I once lived would visit our valley monthly and give a concert under a full moon. The Ozark coyotes had mated with a remnant group of Texas Red Wolves that may explain the twang in the howl. Having provoked the dogs into a frenzy and reminded all humans within hearing distance that the world was still untamed, they would go about their business of raiding nearby chicken houses.

Naturalist and musician, Bernie Krause (2012), believes that animals of different species, types, and shapes make music together in what he calls "the proto-Orchestra" (p. 248), the soundscape of ecology. Wilderness areas have a full orchestra in which various species voices "evolve in concert with one another to accommodate the characteristics of each creature's unique voice" (p. 82). If we listen carefully, we can also hear music in the oceans. Whale songs in which many animals participate occur over long distances and are complex in ways we do not understand (Allen et al., 2018; Payne & McVay, 1971; Rothenberg, 2008; Weintraub, 2019). Whales, in Roger Payne's words (as cited in Whitehead & Rendell, 2015) "give the ocean its voice and the voice they give is ethereal and unearthly" (p. 76). Humpback whale song is:

> long. It cycles with a period sometimes up to thirty minutes, but whales can sing continuously for many hours … the notes are arranged in a very definite way and this structure is what makes a "song" the song of the humpback whale.
>
> (p. 77)

Payne and his colleague, Scott McVay (as cited in Whitehead & Rendell, 2015), have shown that whale song serves multiple functions including the sharing of information, mating, establishing location, and merely saying "hello" (p. 83).

Birds, bugs, coyotes, mammals, and whales, however, are disappearing. The great symphonies of life are going silent as their various members go extinct, as environmentalist Rachel Carson once feared. In the ensuing silence, we might wonder what else we are losing.

In this noisy, fractured, human-dominated world, however, we may not have noticed the disappearance of other species and their music. Our soundscapes are a cacophony of fossil fuel-powered hurry, fear, greed, and the hustle to get the kids to soccer practice. The soundscape of our "developed" civilization is that of a madhouse having neither the evolving order of an intact ecosystem nor that of a symphony orchestra (Mauceri, 2017). We are encased in racket much of the time with psychological effects that we do not understand. For that reason, we might ponder the relationship between our many discontents and dysfunctions and what we hear or what can no longer be heard.

The incessant din of modern life may help to explain why many young people go through their days with earphones attached to their heads. There is, however, no easy escape from the noise of machines, boom boxes, and commercial noise. Someone, long ago, declared war on silence and decided that we will have no relief from inducements, seducements, and distractions all designed to sell us something or prevent us from hearing each other. In the meantime, anger and loneliness are becoming epidemic.

2

From such bits and pieces, I think that we along with bugs, birds, and whales are thoroughly musical. Elena Mannes (as cited in Mauceri, 2017) puts it this way: "Music is encoded in our bodies and brains" (p. 6). It begins between seventeen and nineteen weeks after conception as the fetus, enveloped in a "world of sound, of breath and heartbeat, of rhythm and vibration," develops an auditory system. Great composers build on this early auditory world and in cellist Michael Fitzpatrick's words (as cited in Mauceri, 2017), imitate "natural pulse rates of the way our blood flows, the way our heart beats, the way our brain waves flow" (p. 14). Music can alter our heart rate, blood pressure, breathing, hormones, cortisol levels, and brain waves. Our brain, Mannes (as cited in Mauceri, 2017) believes, is structured to "allow us to experience music both emotionally and physically … the whole brain is a music center" (pp. 28, 33).

Daniel Levitin (2006) argues that making music, indeed, preceded language in our evolution and provided the cognitive development necessary to form language. Levitin (2006) explains it this way:

> Rhythm stirs our bodies. Tonality and melody stir our brains. The coming together of rhythm and melody bridges our cerebellum (the motor control, primitive little brain) and our cerebral cortex (the most evolved, most human part of our brain. (p. 263)

The same, Levitin (2006) believes, may be true for birds and other species.

The upshot is that our affinity for music is inbuilt, woven through our evolution and thoroughly embedded in the brain, mind, and flesh. There is one thing more: we not only live in a world of music but a universe that is "an ocean of sound." Black holes, for example, some 30,000 light years across, "sing" in Mannes's (2011) word as gases are sucked in creating vibrations and pressure waves with an oscillation period of ten million years.

Biologist, E. O. Wilson (1984), makes a similar argument about our ancient affinity for "life and lifelike processes" (p. 1) that he calls "biophilia." We do better, heal faster, think more clearly, and are more creative and healthy in natural settings than in those wholly manmade. Much of the best recent work in landscape and architectural design, accordingly, occurs at the interface between these two poles weaving natural features of daylight, plants, flowing water, and natural materials into buildings, parks, and cityscapes. It would be surprising, indeed, if we did not have an emotional tug toward the waters, plants, animals, and landscapes in which we evolved.

Sacks (2007) believes that "musicophilia is actually a form of biophilia, since music itself feels almost like a living thing" (p. x). It is entirely possible that both musicophilia and biophilia "summon a form of knowing that is deeper than the memory of experience, not fully subject to reason and apparently able to transcend time" (Rosenfeld, 2008, p. 90). What we do know is that both music and natural systems reflect the irreducible beauty in nature. Both are in various ways connected to our physical and mental health. Both are instructive about form, harmony, and design beyond auditory or visual sensation. Both are imbedded in our social rituals, songs, dances, and stories. And, both nature and music energize, inspire, and motivate us. There's the rub.

Both music and love of nature, however, can be perverted to serve causes that destroy larger harmonies. Collective activities such as dancing, song, and rhythmic activities like marching, or what historian William McNeill calls "keeping together in time," have galvanized publics for persecution, war, and conquest throughout history. The Nazi high command at Auschwitz, for instance, were emotionally moved, or perhaps anesthetized, by evening symphony performances. McNeill (1995) adds, however, that they (such activities) "do not need to be harnessed to rival nationalisms of other confrontational identities" (p. 155). "Our future, like our past," he writes, "depends on how we utilize these modes of coordinating common effort" (p. 156). United States history gives many examples of music put to higher purposes. Consider the historic effects of John Newton's, "Amazing Grace,"

Julia Ward Howe's, "Battle Hymn of the Republic," Woody Guthrie's, "This Land is your Land, This Land is My Land," "We Shall Overcome" (writer unknown), John Lennon's "Give Peace a Chance," or the powerful collective experience of concerts in which individual emotions intermingle and amplify through the crowd.

A twisted love of homeland and nature can appeal similarly to a destructive nationalism as evident in the Nazi movement of the 1930s. "By heightening crowd emotions," in Anthony Storr's (1992) words, "music can powerfully contribute to the loss of critical judgement, the blind surrender to the feelings of the moment, with is so dangerously characteristic of crowd behavior" (p. 46). In short, as the Greeks knew long ago, there is nothing automatically benign about either our affinity for music or nature. Those ancient attractors of place, melody, and harmony are very real, but each can be corrupted.

3

The great ecological harmonies that sustain civilization are everywhere under assault. Climate is rapidly becoming less stable and hotter. Oceans are becoming more acidic. Species are disappearing into the void of extinction. The vital signs by which we judge the health of soils, forests, waters, wildlife, and atmosphere are in a rapid downward spiral. The causes are many but, in one way or another, they are the result of the sheer size of the human presence on the planet and a careless state of mind that resembles a kind of autism toward nature. While the warnings from scientists go back many decades, they have not caused enough of us to recognize the face of death or have the foresight to see what lies ahead. United Nations resolutions, scientific declarations, solemn statements of intent, passage of a law here and there, yet further research, another book, another conference, and verbal commitments to do better proliferate like dandelions in the spring. Underlying the hundreds of warnings and the many summons to awaken, is the hope that the market, properly reformed, will become "greener" and internalize its many overlooked costs, or that "breakthrough" technologies will rescue humanity in the nick of time, or that governments will finally pass carbon taxes, so that we can get about our many other preoccupations. I hasten to say that I am for creating an economy fitted to ecological realities along with technology that lessens the human footprint, and smarter public policies and effective governance.

I fear, however, that these are members of the necessary but insufficient family of solutions. Each rests on the quaint belief that we—creatures of biophilia and musicophilia—can be persuaded only by words, rational thinking, cleverness, and more science. And sometimes that is true, but mostly for smaller and more direct threats to our well-being. This time is different.

The scale and duration of our problems are too vast to describe by words or data alone. The deep eternal silence we are bringing about cannot be described or explained logically. In fact, the modern paradigm gives no purely logical reason for *Homo sapiens* to survive its own folly or for Thelma and Louise not to go for that last exciting drive. That leads me to conjecture whether an awakening might come not so much from rationality, but from a deeper reverence, appreciation, and awe that transcend religion and its offspring, which is to say that it will come from the emotional power of music and a deeper experience of nature.

The great educator, John Taylor Gatto, once noticed that first graders, when asked, unanimously and enthusiastically believe that they can sing. The percentage drops year by year until by graduation almost all believe that they have no ability to sing in public and so do not. In the belief that only the well-trained professional can make music, we have become music voyeurs, listening to others perform, attending concerts, and buying CDs while we, the audience, remain mute.

I suspect, however, that there is a great but unsung desire to join the chorus. As evidence, I cite an example from a few years ago when the local TV news filmed Christmas shoppers in a mall interspersed with a choir that began singing the Hallelujah Chorus. After the initial surprise, almost everyone had joined in. The same happens routinely in the seventh inning stretch at a baseball game with the fans singing "Take me out to the ball game." And community choirs and symphonies are a growing and vital part of local culture. In the meantime, school budgets for music education are slashed in the name of fiscal efficiency by those who have no clue while others are lighting bonfires of hate. What's to be done?

In *Songlines*, Bruce Chatwin (1987) describes aboriginal song as "both map and direction finder. Provided that you knew the song, you could always find your way across country" (p. 13). Virtually every part of Australia was included in songlines so that the whole of it could be "read as a musical score." We need something like twenty-first-century songlines to find our way home again, or at least to safe harbor. In this case the question is whether and in what ways music could help us become more compassionate, not just smarter; more sharing, not just richer; kinder, not just more aware of suffering; satisfied, not just bargain shoppers; citizens of the wider world, not just voters; and wiser, not just better informed.

4

In other times, the Greek word "eudaimonia," meaning well-being or human flourishing, would refer to our individual state of mind and soul. In our time it must take on a larger meaning that includes the well-being of all humans, all animals, all ecologies, for all time. In a world with rising seas, larger storms, bigger fires, longer droughts, loss of species, ecological chaos, and the rising likelihood of social and political turmoil, famine, and violence there will not be much eudaimonia, unless we summon the wherewithal to act boldly, wisely, and decisively to change our course. Can music help? If so, how?

Beyond artistry and sheer beauty, music serves many purposes. Properly taught, it may help improve the integration of our unruly selves (Storr, 1992). It is a source of solace in a troubled world (Sacks, 2007). It inspires vision in a world of possibilities. It is a source of reflection and perhaps redemption. Aristotle (as translated by Ernest Barker, 1969) conjectured that "music has some contribution to make to the cultivation of our minds and to the growth of moral wisdom" (p. 340). On occasion, it can move its hearers to seek forgiveness and to forgive. Perhaps it is the pinnacle of human achievement and so a reminder of higher things beyond the tawdry world of self-interest. It can also be used, however, to bamboozle and incite. Whatever its possibilities, "musicking" is, in Christopher Small's (1998) words "a political matter in the widest sense" (p. 13).

But composers and performers alike have been in the forefront of social and political revolutions before. Now, when all that we value and cherish, and all the achievements of humanity are in peril, the only important question for us is what you and I will do about it. For musicians the answer cannot be to more expertly perform a requiem for humanity or flawlessly play the equivalent of one last rendering of "Nearer My God to Thee" on the deck of the Titanic. It must be, rather, to seek new ways of musicking to harness the great powers of musicophilia and biophilia to alert, awaken, and inspire us to defend the habitability of the Earth. To do that, musicians and teachers of music alike might envision themselves as "radical professionals" who see their lives, abilities, and careers hitched to a purpose deeper than artistry (Schmidt, 2000). The examples are many. In *Missa Gaia* and *Grand Canyon*, Paul Winter captured the magnificence of creation, evoking the feelings of awe and reverence we will need to inspire us to extraordinary actions. Michael Fitzpatrick, similarly, in *Earth's Call* is creating musical events aimed to ignite a world-wide response to our predicament—what the Irish might call "a fierce commotion"!

Does this ask too much of musicians, composers, and teachers of music? Most certainly it does, but the same can be said of every profession and every person engaged in defense of life everywhere on Earth. The fact is that we will be redeemed only by heroic efforts that rise to the scale of a moral, spiritual, and social revolution by which humanity will reach a fuller stature.

In the meantime, the rest of us should sing for all we're worth, full-throated singing that comes from deep inside. We should join choirs, spontaneous sing-alongs. We should praise, rock, roll, jump, and shout to the heavens. We should give thanks for the opportunity to live at this particular cross-road of history. When we take a break, we should vote to fund school music programs for every student in every grade. We should demand that Congress begin its otherwise dreary day of serving the oligarchy by loudly singing songs from the progressive era. Perhaps we might ask that great maestro of mischief, Mitch McConnell, to lead a rousing chorus of "We Shall Overcome." What better use of Congress? If not to defend life, justice, beauty, and harmony when it is in peril, what else is music for? … or Congress for that matter?

Notes

1. Solnit (2006) reports the same connection to country music and also cites "Long Black Veil."

References

Allen, J. A., Garland, E. C. Dunlop, R. A., & Noad, M. J. (2018). Cultural revolution reduce complexity in the songs of humpback whales. *Proceeding. Biological Science, 285*(1891), 2018–2088. Doi:10.1098/repb.2018.2088

Aristotle. (1969). *The politics*. E. Barker, Ed. Oxford: Oxford University Press.

Chatwin, B. (1987). *Songlines*. New York: Penguin Books.

Damasio, A. (2018). *The strange order of things*. New York: Pantheon Books.

Kolbert, E. (2014). *The sixth extinction*. New York: Henry Holt.

Krause, B. (2012). *The great animal orchestra*. New York: Little, Brown.

Levitin, D. (2006). *This is your brain on music*. New York: Penguin Books.

Mannes, E. (2011). *The power of music*. New York: Walker and Company.

Mauceri, J. (2017). *Maestros and their music*. New York: Vintage Books.

McGilchrist, I. (2009). *The master and his emissary: The divided brain and the making of the Western world*. New Haven, CT: Yale University Press.

McKibben, B. (2018, November 26). How extreme weather is shrinking the planet. *The New Yorker*. Retrieved from www.newyorker.com/magazine/2018/11/26/how-extreme-weather-is-shrinking-the-planet

McNeill, W. H. (1995). *Keeping together in time*. Cambridge, MA: Harvard University Press.

Midgley, M. (2010, January 1). *The master and his emissary: The divided brain and the making of the Western world* by Iain McGilchrist. *Guardian*. Retrieved from www.theguardian.com/books/2010/jan/02/1

Mora, C., Spirandelli, D., Franklin, E. C., Lynham, J., Kantar, M. B., Miles, W., … Hunter, C. L. (2018). Broad threat to humanity from cumulative climate hazards intensified by greenhouse gas emissions. *Nature Climate Change, 8*(12), 1062–1071. doi:10.1038/s41558–018–0315–6

Orr, D. W. (1992). *Ecological literacy*. Albany, NY: University Press of New York.

Orr, D. W. (2004). *Earth in mind*. Washington, DC: Island Press.

Orr, D. W. (2010). *Hope is an imperative*. Washington, DC: Island Press.

Orr, D. W. (2016). *Dangerous years*. New Haven, CT: Yale University Press.

Payne, R. S., & McVay, S. (1971). Songs of humpback whales. *Science, 173*(3997), 585–597.

Rosenfeld, Z. (2008, June). Feeling and from. *Harper's Magazine,* 89–94.
Rothenberg, D. (2005). *Why birds sing.* New York: Basic Books.
Rothenberg, D. (2008). *Thousand mile song: Whale music in a sea of sound.* New York: Basic Books.
Rothenberg, D. (2013). *Bug music.* New York: St. Martin's Press.
Sacks, O. (2007). *Musicophilia.* New York: Knopf.
Schmidt, J. (2000). *Disciplined minds.* Lanham, MD: Rowman & Littlefield.
Sengupta, S. (2018, August 10). The year global warming turned model into menace. *New York Times.* Retrieved from https://static01.nyt.com/images/2018/08/10/nyt-frontpage/scan.pdf
Small, C. (1998). *Musicking: The meaning of performance and listening.* Middletown, CT: Wesleyan University Press.
Solnit, R. (2006). *A field guide to getting lost.* London: Penguin Books.
Steffen, W., Rockström, J., Richardson, K., Lenton, T.M., Folke, C., Liverman, D., Summerhayes, C.P., … Schellnhuber, H. J. (2018). Trajectories of the earth system in the anthropocene. *Proceedings of the National Academy of Sciences, 115*(33), 8252–8259. doi:10.1073/pnas.1810141115
Storr, A. (1992). *Music and the mind.* New York: Ballantine.
Union of Concerned Scientists. (1992). *World scientists' warning to humanity.* Union of Concerned Scientists. Retrieved from www.ucsusa.org/about/1992-world-scientists.html
U.S. Global Change Research Program (2018). Fourth National Climate Assessment, Volume II, (November, 2018).
Weintraub, K. (2019, January 7). These whales are serenaders of the seas. *New York Times.* Retrieved from www.nytimes.com/2019/01/07/science/whales-songs-acoustics.html
Whitehead, H., & Rendell. L. (2015). *The cultural lives of whales and dolphins.* Chicago, IL: University of Chicago Press.
Wilson, E. O. (1984). *Biophilia.* Cambridge, MA: Harvard University Press.

6 Weaponizing Racism in the Age of Trump

Henry A. Giroux

The utopian visions that support the promise of a radical democracy and prevent the dystopian nightmare of a fascist politics are disappearing in the United States (Giroux, 2016; Levitsky & Ziblatt, 2018). The viciousness of the Trump administration and the cruelty imposed by neoliberalism mutually inform each other. Trump's policies range from stripping food stamps and health care from poor children and caging immigrant children in some god-forsaken prison in Texas to allowing thousands of Puerto Ricans to live for more than a year without electricity, safe water, and decent shelter. Such policies are matched by an ongoing, if not relentless, discourse of dehumanization and objectification aimed at those considered vulnerable and disposable. Notions of the public good are held in disdain matched only by laws and policies that defund public schools, higher education, and other social services in a maelstrom of privatization, deregulation, and corruption. Across the globe, torturers, military dictators, white supremacists, and other political monsters have upended any notion of democracy in the popular imagination. Neoliberalism's machinery of social and political death functions largely to turn everything into a breeding ground for violence, injustice, and misery.

The deep grammar of violence now shapes all aspects of cultural production and becomes visceral in its ongoing production of domestic terrorism, mass shootings, the mass incarceration of people of color, and the war on undocumented immigrants. Not only has it become more gratuitous, random, and in some cases trivialized through the monotony of repetition, it also has become the official doctrine of the Trump administration in shaping its domestic and security policies. Trump's violence has become both promiscuous in its reach and emboldening in its nod to right wing extremist groups. The mix of white nationalism and expansion of policies that benefit the rich, big corporations, and the financial elite are increasingly legitimated and normalized in a new political formation I have called neoliberal fascism (Giroux, 2018a). This new historical conjuncture emerges through a fusion of discredited eugenicist discourses (e.g., Trump's notion you have to be born with the right genes) (OWN, 2016) and a rebooted melange of mythic notions of meritocracy (objective measures of individual quality), scientific racism (pseudo-science that supports racial hierarchies), Horatio Alger fables (anyone can work hard and become rich and successful), and a sheer contempt for the "losers" who are viewed as alien to a white public sphere supported by Trump and his minions (Jones, 2017).

Obsessed with race, Donald Trump has weaponized and racialized the culture wars by using racially charged language and policies to legitimate white supremacist ideologies and pit his supporters against protesting black athletes, undocumented Latino immigrants, dark-skinned immigrants, and other people of color whom he routinely insults and punishes through race-based policies. Trump has claimed that "laziness is a trait in blacks," and called for "a total and complete shutdown of Muslims entering the United States." Meanwhile he stated in December 2015 that a "judge hearing a case about Trump University was biased because of the judge's Mexican heritage." Moreover, he frequently criticizes African-Americans for being unpatriotic, ungrateful and disrespectful." These comments are a small sampling of Trump's racist remarks (Leonhardt & Philbrick, 2018).

Racism runs deep not only in Trump's base but also in a Republican Party that as Paul Krugman points out engages in extreme gerrymandering, voter suppression, voter purges, "deliberate restriction of minority access to the polls," and the ongoing subversion of state legislatures (Krugman, 2018). This is the party that gave us "Strom Thurmond, George H. W. Bush's Willie Horton campaign, or Ronald Reagan's 1980 campaign speech in favor of 'states rights' in a Mississippi town adjacent to the site where three civil-rights workers had been murdered in 1964" (Rich, 2019). In the era of Trump, Frank Rich (2018) goes further and argues, "The Republican Party has proudly and uninhibitedly come out of the closet as the standard-bearer for white supremacy in the Trump era."

What we are witnessing at the current moment is not only the emergence of dangerous illiberal, anti-democratic ideologies that mimic the legacy of white nationalism but also the resurgence of a powerful affective and educational culture nurtured by false promises, anger, feelings of repulsion, hatred, and the spectacularization of violence. What is alarming about this culture of intolerance, bigotry, and violence is its alignment with the Nazi obsession with notions of cultural and biological pollution and their systemic efforts to purge society of those deemed contaminated. This language is not unlike Trump's characterization of asylum seekers as vermin, who will bring "large-scale crime and disease" to the United States (Da Silva, 2018).

The merging of neoliberalism and elements of a fascist playbook are now anchored firmly in the language of disposability and pollution. This rhetoric is part of a representational crisis marked by the increasing attraction of and growth of architectures of meaning and proliferating digital platforms and cultural apparatuses engaged in the production of modes of desire, identifications, and values that fuel a right wing or apocalyptic populism. The current historical conjuncture is marked by a new era of politics and way of thinking about place, community, rootlessness, and identity. The once dominant narratives about critical agency, truth, justice, and democracy are collapsing. Fascist terror is no longer fixed in the past or ephemeral to the twenty-first century. Under the Trump administration, malice, lies, and unrelenting cruelty have become official policy and fraught with dangerous risks. Fascist politics avoids reason, maligns the truth, and appeals to a pathological nationalism. In doing so it creates a mythic past that either denigrates or excludes those considered at odds with its notions of white supremacy and racial purity. What emerges is a celebration of the brutality of 1930s, which becomes a signpost for imagining a present under what Trump's nostalgically codes in the slogans "America First" and "Make America Great Again." Culture now becomes integral to a politics deeply rooted in an anti-democratic ethos.

Under neoliberalism, a new political formation has developed in which a racialist worldview merges with the economic dictates of a poisonous form of casino capitalism. Echoes of the past can be heard in Trump and his associates' repeated use of a language boiling over with terms such as "vermin," "animals," "stupid," and "losers" to name only a few of the toxic expressions crucial to a politics of social cleansing, racial purity, and violent forms of exclusion. The current language of disposability and pollution carries with it powerful affective overtones that "transform the noble concept of a common humanity into a disdainful sneer" (Etlin, 2002, p. 3) if not worse.

The language of pollution is used to treat some groups as not simply inferior but also as a threat to the body politic, and is closely aligned with the language of camps and extermination. More than an ostentatious display of power on the part of the Trump administration, the language of pollution and disposability functions as a performative language designed to dramatize and re-enact national identity, one that defines itself in white nationalist assumptions. Assigned to the dumping ground of social and political abandonment, those individuals or families considered noxious and superfluous are now associated with a rootlessness that bears a close resemblance to the Nazi notion of blood and soil. Looking back at the Nazi era, the dangers of the language of disposability and pollution become terrifying given how they were deployed in the interest of unimaginable horrors. Professor Richard A. Etlin (2002) provides a glimpse of the logic and effects of the discourse of pollution and its morphing into policies of disposability and eradication. He writes:

> From propaganda posters to problems in mathematics textbooks for schoolchildren, Germans were repeatedly asked, once the Nazis had come to power, to ponder the economic costs of maintaining the lives of the handicapped and mentally ill. Forced sterilization of people

> considered "hereditarily ill" had been decreed in July 1933; compulsory abortions, in 1935. The legalized secret killing of deformed and retarded children began in 1939, as did plans for the murder of Germany's adult mental patients, both programs "planned and administered by medical professionals" involving "some of Germany's oldest and most highly respected hospitals." The utilitarian calculation of the cost of sustaining life for these so-called unproductive members of German society does not account for the full reasoning behind such measures. Rather, one must look to an altered moral outlook best represented by the notion of the "Vernichtung lebensunwerten Lebens," that is, the "destruction" or "extermination," of "lives not worth living".
>
> (p. 3)

The politics of disposability is no longer a discourse limited to the historical memory of totalitarian governments, internment camps, and extermination policies. As both a state-legitimated ideology and established policy, it now exists at the highest levels of the U. S. government and is central to the creation of a death-saturated age. Fantasies of absolute control, racial cleansing, unchecked militarism, and class warfare are at the heart of an American imagination that has turned lethal. This dystopian mindset is marked by hollow words and lethal actions; similarly, its dreamscape is pillaged of any substantive meaning, cleansed of compassion, and used to legitimate the notion that alternative worlds are impossible to entertain. In this worldview, the present creates nightmares parading as dreams in which the future is imagined "by way of a detour through a mythic past" (Thompson, 2018). There is more at stake here than shrinking political horizons and the aligning of the existing moment with echoes of a fascist past (Giroux, 2018b). What we are witnessing is a mode of governing fueled by fantasies of exclusion accompanied by a full-scale attack on morality, thoughtful reasoning, and collective resistance rooted in democratic forms of struggles. We are also witnessing an unprecedented assault on the mainstream media and the fundamental necessity in a democracy for an independent, critical journalism.

The question of what the role of higher education is in a time of tyranny has to be situated within the current historical moment when neoliberal fascism is on the march and has produced a wide-ranging shift in the economy, ideology, power, culture, and politics. Ways of imagining society through the lens of democratic ideals, values, and social relations have given way to narratives that substitute cruelty for compassion, greed for generosity, and pollution for social bonds rooted in human rights. The language of disposability and pollution has become the new mantra not just for an assault on human rights but also as a warning and unapologetic forecast of the horrors of state power and its turn to a politics of social and racial cleansing, along with its embrace of authoritarianism. We face in the current era a major challenge to education, reason, and informed judgment and their relationship to democracy. The formative cultures necessary to ensure the production of informed and critical citizens necessary for a democracy are collapsing under the weight of the powers of the financial elite and big corporations. We live at a time when fascism is on the table and has become a driving, if not commanding force, in American politics. This is particularly evident in the ways in which particular children become subject to a politics of disposability.

Beyond a Politics of Objectification

In the age of Trump, children of undocumented workers are stripped of their humanity, caged in internment camps, sometimes sexually abused and subjected to the unethical grammars of state violence. Sometimes they lose their lives, as did two children from Guatemala who died while in custody of Customs and Border Protection: seven-year-old Jakelin Caal and eight-year-old Felipe Gomez. In this way the dual logic of disposability and pollution becomes the driving force of a machinery of social death.

Removed from the sphere of justice and human rights, undocumented children occupy a ruthless space of social and political abandonment beyond the reach of human rights. This is a zone in which moral numbness becomes a central feature of politics, power, and governance. How else to explain Republican Congressman Peter King responding to the deaths of these two children by praising ICE's "excellent record," stating that since there are "only two children that have died," the death count is a testament to how competent organizations like ICE actually are (Darby, 2018). This is a fascist discourse marked by the rhetorical tropes of hate, demonization, and violence.

As a form of domestic terrorism, the state produces and legitimates in both its policies and its alignment with corporate controlled media, forms of material and symbolic violence in which people are rendered less than human, treated as excess, and subjected to zones of social abandonment and terminal exclusion. Such terrorism is at the heart of the Trump administration and is evident in its anti-immigration policies, its militarization of the southern border, its expansion of the surveillance state, and its war on Muslims. It is also evident in mounting police violence against black youth, its revocation of DACA, its attack on workers' rights and safety protections, its creation of internment camps near the U.S. Mexico border, its scorn for women's reproductive rights, and its elevation of the police state as a central force for organizing society to name only a few examples.

Disposable populations now labor under what Richard Sennett (2007) has called the "spectre of uselessness" and are catapulted out of the moral universe central to any notion of humanity. Such populations have their children forcibly taken away from them by immigration officials, are chased out of their homes, forced into exile, pushed into homelessness and poverty, excluded from the rights that grant them full-fledged citizenship. Too many of the poor and other vulnerable populations are frequently left to fend for themselves in the face of often devastating political and social costs caused by the financial elite and exploitative corporations such as the pharmaceutical companies partly responsible for the opioid crisis in the United States. These vulnerable populations are also removed from their material goods, crucial social provisions, and lack control over their bodies. Such populations under the reign of neoliberalism are viewed with scorn, disdain, and have a social death forced upon them in lieu of a real death.

Disposability, pollution, and dispossession have another lethal register in that they attempt through a range of cultural, social, and pedagogical apparatuses to make people unknown to themselves as potentially critical and engaged citizens. As public spheres increasingly become sites where politics thrive on the energies of a racially coded fascist politics, critical modes of subjectivity and identification are under siege. That is, new powerful cultural pathways work to choke democratic values, modes of agency, values, and social relations normally rooted in the virtues of social and economic justice, compassion for others, and also the public goods and institutions that make such values and relationships possible. Critical thinking, civic courage, and collective resistance are diverted into the private orbit of therapy, the isolated space of emotional management, the atomizing logic of wilful self-change, and a landscape of fractured identities.

Neoliberal ideology becomes a justification for lawlessness when responsibility is shifted to the most vulnerable individuals, with women being disproportionally burdened as they are marginalized by class and race. Even though the problems faced by the dispossessed are not of their own making, the poisoned discourse of neoliberalism insists that their fate is a product of personal issues ranging from weak character, bad choices, or simply a moral deficiency. Isolation breeds political impotence, fear, and intimidation, which work not only to instil toxic convictions but also "to destroy the capacity to form any" (Arendt, 1951, p. 468) In this discourse, everyone is defined as an island and all connective forms of economic and social justice vanish from the public imagination.

As misfortune is emptied of any broader political, economic, and social content, it is indeed depoliticized and viewed as a weakness, hence making it all the easier for the punishing state to criminalize social problems. As the late Frankfurt School theorist Leo Löwenthal (1987) once noted, terror functions as a form of dehumanization and "fate itself becomes so enigmatic as to lose all meaning. … The creative faculties of fantasy, imagination, memory become meaningless and tend to atrophy where they can no longer bring about any desired change in the individual's fate" (pp. 182–183). One consequence is that those individuals who are relatively powerless to address broader social issues are forced to partake in a system that encourages them to embrace their own oppression as though it were a normal part of their everyday existence.

Operating under the false assumption that there are only individual solutions to socially-produced problems, the atomization of the individual thus becomes normalized, rendering human beings numb and fearful, immune to the demands of economic and social justice increasingly divorced from matters of politics, ethics, and social responsibility. This amounts to a form of domestic terrorism evident as individuals descend into a moral stupor, susceptible to political shocks, and seduced by the pleasure of the manufactured spectacle. In this instance not only does the political become relentlessly personal, it also reinforces the ongoing process of depoliticization. In this case, agency is reduced to a dystopian narrative limited to how to survive, dumbs down the notion of autonomy to acts of consumption, allowing any aspirations that regain some sense of sovereignty to be hijacked by right-wing parties and populist movements. Neither Trump's rise nor the emergence of right-wing populism happened in a vacuum. Trump built on a longstanding neoliberal project buttressed by an anti-democratic formative culture in which educational institutions have been used to shape market-based identities, modes of agency and collective subjects bound together by the notion that there is no alternative to an unfair and pernicious capitalist social order.

Beyond Capitalist Realism

In response to this argument, the late radical blogger Mark Fisher (2009) coined the term "capitalist realism." As he explains in his book on that topic, the term describes "the widespread sense that not only is capitalism the only viable political and economic system, but also that it is now impossible even to imagine a coherent alternative to it" (p. 2). For Fisher, capitalist realism functioned less as a crude form of quasi-propaganda than as a pedagogical, social and cultural machine that produces "a pervasive atmosphere, conditioning not only the production of culture but also the regulation of work and education, and acting as a kind of invisible barrier constraining thought and action" (Fisher, 2009, p. 16). Hidden behind an unquestioned anonymity, neoliberalism appears less as an ideology than as a market-based rationality that by default rightly rejects any inquiry into its goal of governing all of social life. Neoliberalism's unforgiving logic of globalization attempts to make its own power invisible while making people prisoners of its privatizing, commodifying, mutilating ode to self-interest and hyper-individualism.

What Fisher wisely understood was that any resistance to neoliberal capitalism would have to engage education as a central feature of politics, especially as a way to challenge neoliberal common sense and the pedagogical apparatuses that produce it. Borrowing from the work of Antonio Gramsci,

Raymond Williams, C. Wright Mills, and others, Fisher addressed this issue by expanding the meaning of education far beyond the notion of established schooling and pointed to popular culture, the arts, science, film, journalism, social media, and other sites of cultural production as the lens through which to both imagine an alternative to global capitalism and to mobilize individual and collective forms of resistance to it. In this instance, culture, if not the very notion of populism, becomes a site of struggle rather than a terrain grounded exclusively in the grip of domination. In the current situation, as Chantal Mouffe (2016) observes, it is crucial to discard the notion that populism is simply another form of demagogy. On the contrary, she writes, "it is a way of doing politics which can take various forms, depending on the periods and the places. It emerges when one aims at building a new subject of collective action—the people—capable of reconfiguring a social order lived as unfair," and in need of a defense of freedom, social justice, and equality.

What does it mean to challenge the pedagogical assumptions that inform neoliberalism, who are the agents to do so, where will such struggles take place, and what form will the language of criticism and hope look like if it is to address the everyday lives of people caught in the grip of neoliberal common-sense? Neoliberalism has created a crisis of agency, representation, and resistance, and all of these elements must be addressed in terms of how they both function in a neoliberal order to undermine democracy and what it would mean to develop a language and mode of analysis capable of rethinking these issues as part of a comprehensive understanding of politics and collective struggles. We must also ask how the right wing and demagogue politicians were able to colonize populist aspirations to regain some control over the political process and why the left failed. Shaming those who follow Trump is a failing political strategy, especially since many of his followers have suffered under neoliberal globalization and while confused politically, are not in agreement with the neoliberal project. Rather than demonize Trump and his followers, a new political strategy suggests reclaiming the promise of a radical democracy, and exploring how such an ideal is undermined and attacked in a neoliberal order in which everything is privatized, commodified, deregulated, and organized as part of the culture of commercialism and subject to the dictates of finance capital.

Such a challenge would demand developing modes of education and critical analysis that examine in accessible and rigorous modes of expression how power is used by ruling elites to exploit, exclude, dehumanize, and undermine any viable mode of critical agency. It would call into question the methods through which the state, corporations, and the financial elite use power to remove from people's lives essential services such as health care, public transportation, free quality education, housing, a social wage, healthy environment, and other services that enable people to expand their capacities as critically-engaged, joyful agents. I am not suggesting that all conservative politicians, including right-wing elements of the Democratic Party such as the Clinton/Obama wing, support the same reactionary policies embraced by Trump and his followers. In fact, Democratic Party politicians from Clinton and Obama to Feinstein and Pelosi actually profess to be a counter force to Trump—often labelling themselves as the party of resistance—but in the long run, they end up supporting policies and power relations that favour the ruling elites. Under such circumstances, these alleged "liberal" politicians, not unlike the German-Socialists in the Weimer Republic, turned their back on the needs of workers, the poor, minorities of class and color, and in doing so helped to create a populist revolt that supported the anti-elitist, anti-government discourse on which Trump ran his presidential campaign.[1]

Any viable notion of politics has to consider working through a variety of cultural apparatuses to activate a public imagination willing to fight for institutions and public goods capable of revitalizing social bonds, social responsibility, and the capacity for experiences that go beyond the narrow notions of individualism and self-interest celebrated in the neoliberal worldview. It is both a political and pedagogical issue to imagine a future in which human needs take precedent over market considerations, while making clear how capitalism with its concentration of wealth and power in few hands produces modes of inequality and human misery. The agents and modes of resistance necessary for defeating capitalism and constructing a democratic socialist order will not emerge without the production of a formative culture that provides the knowledge, ideas, values, and social relations central to creating engaged citizens. Sites of such struggle include not only higher education, but also public education, the arts, social services, the social media, religious institutions, and those other domains of cultural production capable of utilizing the voices and work of public intellectuals. At stake here is the challenge for educators and other cultural workers to own up to the complexity of the problems capitalism produces, to write and speak to people in a narrative that they can understand and identify with, and to address what it means to make knowledge, images, and ideas meaningful in order to make them critical and emancipatory.

The issue of how ordinary Americans can be motivated to be self-reflective, moved by democratic values while embracing relationships marked by shared responsibilities, begins with a language in which people can be moved emotionally, spiritually, and intellectually to analyze their problems and their relationship to broader social forces. One task of such a language is to awaken people's capacity to align themselves with collective identities steeped in communal bonds, develop a compassion for others, and identify with the public good. Such a language has to replace state-sanctioned fear with a radical notion of what Ronald Aronson (2017) describes in his book *We: Reviving social hope* as "social hope"—a hope that moves people not only to imagine a different future but to individually and collective act on it.

The economic crisis produced under neoliberalism has been matched by a crisis of ideas. This suggests that at the heart of neoliberal capitalism and its fascist politics is a crisis of representation, agency, and memory. In part, this crisis was captured by the phrase attributed to Fredrick Jameson or Slavoj Zizek that "it is easier to imagine the end of the world than it is to imagine the end of capitalism" (Jameson, 2003). This dystopian assessment challenges us to redefine and rethink the politics that produced it. Doing so would require not only interrogating the current crisis of neoliberal fascism, but also thinking about the promise of a radical democracy.

John Dewey, Vaclav Havel, and others have long warned us that a simplistic faith in the stability of the institutions in which a democracy is grounded will not automatically prevent the emergence of authoritarianism. But authoritarian societies are not just the result of bad governance, but more importantly emerge from a more fundamental deformation in the culture itself. That is, democracy's survival depends on a formative culture whose strength lies in a set of habits and dispositions rooted in a civic culture and literacy capable of sustaining it. The deep-seated habits of cruelty, greed, consumerism, racism, and unchecked individualism at the heart of neoliberal fascism are eroding the social fabric that make a democracy possible. Coercion, fear, and repression are not the only tools used by authoritarian societies. Matters of value, identity, agency, and the habits of solidarity when in crisis are as threatening to a democracy as are the forces of repression. Ignorance is the mortar and building blocks of fascism. Politics follows culture, and this means that an informed public is central to any democracy and being informed points to addressing how the habits of democracy as part of a broader understanding of education and the institutions that sustain it can be protected. We have no time to waste.

Note

1. I want to thank the always brilliant Michael Lerner for helping me clarify this point.

References

Arendt, H. (1951). *The origins of totalitarianism.* Prague: Schocken Books.

Aronson, R. (2017). *We: Reviving social hope*. Chicago, IL: University of Chicago Press.

Da Silva, C. (2018, December 11). Donald Trump says migrants bring "large scale crime and disease" to America. *Newsweek.* Retrieved from: www.newsweek.com/donald-trump-says-migrants-bring-large-scale-crime-and-disease-america-1253268

Darby, L. (2018, December 29). GOP Congressman calls two children dying in border detention an "excellent record". *GQ Magazine*. Retrieved from: www.gq.com/story/peter-king-dead-kids-excellent

Etlin, R. A. (2002). *Art, culture, and media under the Third Reich.* Chicago, IL: University of Chicago Press. p. 3.

Fisher, M. (2009). *Capitalist realism: Is there no alternative?* Winchester: Zero Books.

Giroux, H. A. (2016). *America at war with itself.* San Francisco, CA: City Lights Books.

Giroux, H. A. (2018a, June 10). The nightmare of Neoliberal fascism. *Truthout.* Retrieved from: https://truthout.org/articles/henry-a-giroux-the-nightmare-of-neoliberal-fascism/

Giroux, H. A. (2018b). *American nightmare: Facing the challenge of fascism.* San Francisco, CA: City Lights Books.

Jameson, F. (2003, May-June). Future city. *New Left Review*. Retrieved from: https://newleftreview.org/II/21/fredric-jameson-future-city

Jones, S. (2017, February 15). Trump has turned the GOP into the party of eugenics. *The New Republic*. Retrieved from: https://newrepublic.com/article/140641/trump-turned-gop-party-eugenics

Krugman, P. (2018, December 10). The G.O.P. goes full authoritarian. *New York Times*. Retrieved from: www.nytimes.com/2018/12/10/opinion/trump-gop-authoritarian-states-power-grab.html

Leonhardt, D., & Philbrick, I. P. (2018, January 15). Donald Trump's racism: The definitive list. *New York Times.* Retrieved from: www.nytimes.com/interactive/2018/01/15/opinion/leonhardt-trump-racist.html

Levitsky, S., & Ziblatt, D. (2018). *How democracies die.* New York: Crown.

Löwenthal, L. (1987). *False prophets: Studies in authoritarianism*. New Brunswick, NJ: Transaction Books.

Mouffe, C. (2016, November 21). The populist moment. *Open Democracy.* Retrieved from www.opendemocracy.net/democraciaabierta/chantal-mouffe/populist-moment

OWN. (2016, March 22). *Donald Trump on the role genetics play in success | The Oprah Winfrey Show | Oprah Winfrey Network* [Video file]. Retrieved from: www.youtube.com/watch?v=YclB7UDbnKQ

Rich, F. (2018, November 29). Mueller's steady stream of Russia revelations is driving Trump crazy. *New York.* Retrieved from: http://nymag.com/intelligencer/2018/11/mueller-revelations-drive-trump-crazy.html

Rich, F. (2019, January 17). With State of the Union disinvitation, Pelosi outmaneuvers Trump once again. *New York.* Retrieved from: http://nymag.com/intelligencer/2019/01/frank-rich-pelosi-outmaneuvers-trump-on-sotu-disinvitation.html

Sennett, R. 2007. *The culture of the new capitalism*. New Haven, CN: Yale University Press.

Thompson, A. K. (2018, December 10). Premonitions: Fragments of a culture of revolt. *Socialist Project: The Bullet*. Retrieved from: https://socialistproject.ca/2018/12/premonitions-fragments-of-culture-of-revolt/

7 An Ecology of Eudaimonia and its Implications for Music Education

June Boyce-Tillman

This chapter explores the Greek origins of eudaimonia and the way it has been developed by theologians such as Thomas Aquinas and psychologists such as Abraham Maslow and Carl Rogers and gives examples of musical educational projects designed to express these values.

Ancient Greek philosophy

"Eudaimonia" has been adapted for various purposes over centuries. In the world of Plato and Aristotle (Ackrill, 1981), it described virtuous living—a life not purely devoted to pleasure, but one in which emotions are controlled by reason. The three elements in Aristotle's thinking were virtue, wisdom, and flourishing (including the physical body). Behaving ethically was seen as being truthful, beautiful, and good (Boyce-Tillman, 2016a). So, the eudaimonic person, according to Aristotelian ethics, is harmonious within the self and exhibits virtues such as justice, piety, courage, self-control, and wisdom to create a harmonious society. Eudaimonia is seen as the essence of being fully human.

The word in Greek, combined *eu*—meaning well—with *daimon* which could be seen as having a good indwelling spirit—daimon or soul—which was linked with the idea of fulfilling the purpose for one's life. It could also be read as being in good relationship with good spirits or ancestors. Aristotle saw friendship as a consequence of eudaimonia and the satisfaction produced by relationships which are mutual and respectful

Medieval Theology

In 1246–7 Aristotle's *Nicomachean Ethics* was published in a Latin translation by Richard Grosseteste and provoked Thomas Aquinas's *Sententia libri Ethicorum* (Donato, 2007), a Christianizing of Aristotle's concept of eudaimonia. Whereas Aristotle saw the purpose of human nature as ethical behaviour, Aquinas added the idea of the beatific vision seen only dimly in this life and complete in heaven. To the natural, moral, socio-political, and temporary eudaimonia of Aristotle, he added theological, supernatural, ontological transcendence. From these origins, the field of virtue ethics has grown; concepts in eudaimonia such as excellence, practical (including physical) or moral wisdom, balance, and contemplation have been recontextualized in a variety of ways.

Positive Psychology

The questioning of Christian belief and two world wars intervened between Aquinas and the twenty-first century. The search for life's meaning took new forms. The positive psychology movement, based on Aristotelian ideas, was concerned with what enables human beings to function well in biological, personal, relational, institutional, cultural, and global dimensions (Seligman & Csikszentmihalyi, 2000). Thinkers now drew from Maslow's (1962) hierarchy of human needs which (usually drawn as a pyramid) included the basic physical needs for food, water, air and safety, the psychological needs for love, belonging (relationships) and esteem (feelings of achievement), and the fulfillment need for self-actualization (realizing one's potential including creativity). Later Maslow (1970a, 1970b) added the needs for cognitive understanding (knowledge and curiosity) and aesthetic experience (beauty, order, symmetry), and, beyond self-actualization, the transcendent, often called peak experiences. The possibility of transcendence within the musical experience has been seen as the last remaining place for the soul in Western society (Argyle, 1997; Kung, 1992). These so-called peak experiences included characteristics previously associated with the soul: an intense experience of the present, concentration, self-forgetfulness, a lessening of defences and inhibitions, empowerment, trust, spontaneity, euphoria, joy, wonder, and a fusion of a person with the world. Maslow did see educational implications for his model, setting up a vision of humanist education that would produce people who:

> would take their own lives into their hands to a greater extent. With increased personal responsibility for one's personal life, and with a rational set of values to guide one's choosing, people would begin to actively change the society in which they live.
>
> (Maslow, 1971, p. 195)

American psychologists, such as Carl Rogers (1976), located eudaimonia in inward exploration, similar to Aquinas's notion of contemplation, but now situated within the self rather than in a territory (heaven) beyond it. Eudaimonia became harnessed in the pursuit of long-term peace and contentment, through finding meaning and purpose. Happiness (as in Aristotle's "flourishing") is seen as a temporary emotion and eudaimonia as an ongoing state of being.

From a combination of ancient Greek philosophy, medieval ideas, and positive psychology many people in the later twentieth century have developed wellbeing programs. Carol Ryff (1989) developed the six-factor model of psychological wellbeing, including self-acceptance, personal growth, purpose in life, environmental mastery, autonomy, and positive relations with other people. Martin Seligman in *Flourish* (2011) set out the PERMA model of wellbeing, which included positive emotion, engagement, positive relationships, meaning and accomplishment/achievement. This included the very popular concept of resilience, connected with autonomy and power. From all these bases, governments have attempted to measure wellbeing,[1] including the eudemonic.[2]

Contemporary Views of "Wellbeing"

In current examinations of eudaimonia, new elements appear, such as with Rowan Williams (2017) who sees eudaimonia residing in a right relationship with the body, the natural world, the social world, and the cosmos. Partha Choudhury (2011), in an orientation for a possible future culture and civilization (pp. 87–95), includes eco-activism, spirituality (with a sense of meaning and purpose and positive core values), social networks (including embracing different cultures), and nurturing. So, from the past and the present, we can infer eudaimonic dispositions and abilities:

1. Ethical behavior (including toward the self and the environment)
2. Relationships of mutuality, respect (including nurture)
3. Autonomy (including positive core values on which to make informed decisions)
4. A sense of meaning and purpose (which may include a cosmic dimension)
5. Contemplation (which may or may not include a sense of a higher power beyond the world)
6. Relationship with spirits of the ancestors and celestial beings (which can be part of the peak experience)

The rest of the chapter will examine how these can be related to the musical experience and music education.

A Phenomenography of Music

These themes can be related to a phenomenographic map of the musical experience. This describes:

> the varying ways of experiencing that phenomenon … in relation to the particular features of diverse awarenesses … This is a shift from individual awareness that varies as to focus and simultaneous awareness of aspects of a phenomenon to a collective awareness in which all such variations can be seen. (Marton & Booth, 1997, pp. 108–9)

This phenomenographic map (Figure 7.1) of music (Boyce-Tillman, 2016a) is drawn from numerous accounts of the musical experience:

- The way the phenomenon is reviewed in research traditions
- How it appears in the literature, treatises and textbooks of different cultures
- Discourses and accounts of musical experiences

The map identifies interacting domains within the musical experience:

> The variation between different ways of experiencing something, then, derives from the fact that different aspects of different parts of the whole may or may not be discerned and be objects of focal awareness simultaneously … The unit of phenomenographic research … is an internal relationship between the experiencer and the experienced.
>
> (Marton & Booth, 1997, pp. 112–13)

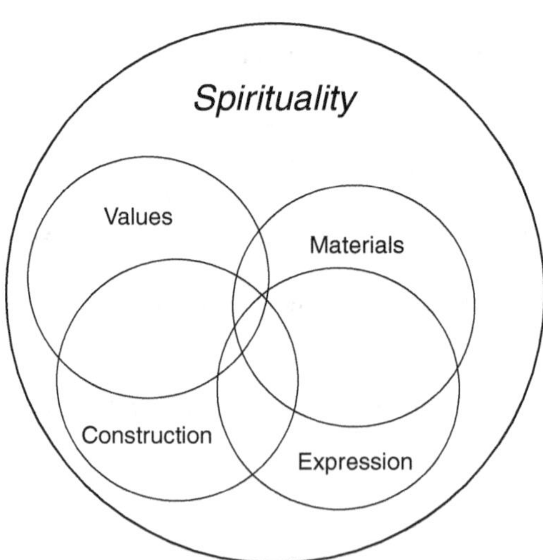

Figure 7.1 A Phenomenographic Map of the Spiritual Experience in Music.

Music education has traditionally concentrated on only a few of the domains, yet all need addressing to understand how various aspects of eudaimonia are linked with music:

- Materials—the instruments, the body and the technical aspects involved in producing sound as well as the acoustics of the space
- Expression—the feelingful aspects of the experience including those within the sounds themselves (intrinsic) and those locked onto the sounds by significant life experiences (extrinsic)
- Construction—the way music is put together—what is repeated, what is changed, the degree of contrast
- Values—the context of musicking and its cultural meaning
- Spirituality/liminality—a different way of knowing where time and space operate differently

The diversity of these domains indicates the breadth and depth of the musical experience, and therefore, its potential to cover the diverse aspects of eudaimonia. The rest of this chapter will consider how these might be encouraged in music education.

Ethical Behavior to Self and Environment

Music consists of organizations of concrete materials drawn both from the human body and the environment. These include musical instruments of various kinds, the infinite variety of tone colors associated with the human voice and the sounds of the natural world. While instrumental technique has concentrated on the movement of one part of the body, such as the fingers on the piano, more recent studies reveal an increasing interest in this area. Chanda and Levitin (2013) in *The Neurochemistry of Music*, explore the use of music not only to regulate mood and arousal in everyday life but also to promote physical and psychological health and wellbeing in clinical settings, through the engagement of neurochemical systems first for reward, motivation, and pleasure; second for stress and arousal; third for immunity; and finally, for social affiliation, all relating to concepts in Aristotle and Aquinas. For example, Clift et al. (2013) explore the feasibility of weekly community singing for people with Chronic Pulmonary Disorder assessing the positive impact on lung function (Morrison & Clift, 2012).

The close relation to the natural world has also similarly been ignored until recently along with the acoustic space (Abrams, 1996; Boyce-Tillman, 2010). Ecological understanding could be transformed if, for example, violin students were taught to open their violin cases and honor the tree that gave its life for the instrument. In traditional societies, the player would regard him or herself as continually in relationship to that tree. Our industrialized society with its production lines for musical instruments dislocates the connection between the natural world and the materials of sound.

Emotions and Music

The domain of musical expression is where emotion and feeling are explored. Eudaimonia includes the management of emotional states. The experiences of the composer/performer and listener interact here to give a variety of truths derived from the interplay between the intrinsic (in the music itself) and extrinsic (meaning that has been locked onto that particular piece or style or musical tradition because of its association with certain events) (Green, 1988, 1997). This has often been downplayed by classical theorists (Rahn, 1994, p. 55), but it is where the hidden aspects of personality or psyche reside—the inner self or daimon. Here is a domain where poetry, story, and biography can inform understanding and illuminate the area of personal significance such as the linkage of Beethoven's Heiligenstadt Testament (in which he is angry about his hearing loss) with works like his Fifth Symphony. Insights from music therapy can be used here, but differently in the context of education:

> The facilitation of the process aims towards a deeper inner self-exploration rather than therapeutic attendance to the participants' psychopathological needs. This relationship is interpersonal and inter-psychic, happening verbally or non-verbally with the whole group and each individual separately.
>
> (Batzoglou, 2011, n/p)

The personal emotional conflict involved in creativity is seen by some writers as potentially resolved through an act of regression (Boyce-Tillman, 2016a, pp. 81–122) in which we recover our aesthetic modes of structuring experience. Like the title of Witkin's book, *The Intelligence of Feeling* (1974), this is very much in line with Aristotle's concept of virtue being emotion in relation with reason. The presence of composing/improvising in the current music education curriculum in England enables students to learn this skill as a way of coming to peace within themselves. For example, the mother of a very bright girl was diagnosed with terminal brain cancer. She started by writing a piano trio called *Winter*. It was a bleak piece full of sadness and emptiness. Two years later, when her mother had died, she listened to her piece and said insightfully: "I don't like it, but it says what I wanted it to say." Classroom composing could help a young person deal with grief.

Virtues and Music Education

Plato linked music and virtues, although it does not appear often in contemporary literature. However, in a study of spirituality in music education—coming from a former communist state, Lithuania—Arvydas Girdzijauskas (2017) sets out to show the relationship of music education (including performing music, learning music language and theory, improvising, arranging, and listening to and interpreting music) to certain virtues. He demonstrates how children involved in active musical practice are more skilled in managing their emotions. Rather than analyzing the academic benefits of music education (Winner & Hetland, 2000), he concentrates on emotional reactions (Piliciauskas, 1998) and social relations (Bastian, 2000).

Relationships

Aristotle saw eudaimonia as resulting in relationships that are mutual and respectful. The clearest exponent of this is Nel Noddings (1984, 1992) in her setting out of an ethics of care. Central to Noddings's thinking is that "caring-about," or the notion of justice, common to Plato and Aristotle, must underpin classroom practice to engender an atmosphere in which "caring-for" can flourish (Noddings, 2002, pp. 23–4). This she describes as a reciprocal relationship between two human beings and critiques the abstraction, assessment driven, and individualized contemporary models of education. She sees caring as a way of repairing our world. It has both personal, social, and cosmic significance. Olivia Dowd (2019) describes Noddings's thinking as applied to the music classroom:

> Music teaches empathy and compassion. There is truth in music, and in music we hear courage, love, faith, kindness—a spectrum of emotions and ideas. However, educating people about music and with music does not always include conversations about the effects that music can have. It can be in the delivery of music teaching that we see the gaping hole of humanity versus performance product. At the heart of every piece of music is a person, but in the classroom, we are more often concerned with the product and the process rather than the human that created the piece we are playing, the emotions invoked, or the actual humans playing the piece.
>
> (p. 278)

Sarah Morgan (Morgan & Boyce-Tillman, 2016, pp. 96–8) looks at the leadership styles necessary to create mutual relationships within a community choir. These include the skills traditionally supported in music training, such as the *conductor*. Other roles, however, such as the *catalyst*, concern a desire to create change, a focus on community (Pascale, 2005) with an understanding of group dynamics, balancing challenge and support, and with an inclusive approach. The *organizer* pays attention to maintaining system and order, with strengths in the area of administration and management. Values underpin the role of the *muse*, who is concerned with the long-term wellbeing of the musical group. The roles of *muse* and *catalyst* demand a high level of empathy and interpersonal skills, while those of the *conductor* and *organizer* involve close attention to detail and technicality. Leaders of groups in music educational contexts need to acquire a similar range of personal relational characteristics rather than purely musical skills.

At Winchester University, a project called Music Lessons on Prescription (Walker & Boyce-Tillman, 2002), examines the role of music lessons in the treatment of children diagnosed with chronic anxiety, anticipating the current development in the UK of social prescribing. One pupil was off all his antidepressants and running his own rock group after three months of drumming lessons. He had been out of school and on medication for two years. Musical relationships can have a significant effect on empathy and mutuality. Too much individual assessment does not encourage this potential.

This domain also encompasses the use of music in reconciliation between cultures (Urbain, 2007), an area of social significance. Musicians working in the area of cultural fusion look toward music as a route to justice and peace (Boyce-Tillman, 1996, 2001a, 2007c), such as Paul Simon in his recording *Graceland* in the context of apartheid in South Africa (Simon, 1994).

Alice Miller (1987) saw violence potentially transformed by creativity. There was one London school in which discipline had broken down. A new head was appointed to turn the school around. One of her strategies was to give the dissident ring leaders drumming lessons. They now became the leaders of the school's musicking rather than of its rebellion. Their violence was channelled and contained by musical engagement.

Reason and Emotion

Typically, in the Academy, rationality and order are brought into contact with emotional content (as prized by Aristotle), originating in a "personal need to create order and wholeness" (Kemp, 1996, p. 216) in the face of internal conflicts and stresses. The emphasis in musicology has been on the literate Western classical tradition, downplaying orate musical cultures, which have, perhaps, a more immediate relationship to current feeling. In this way the concept of "The Beautiful" became limited and culturally confined. It has meant the marginalization of improvisatory elements with their delight in spontaneity, play, and immediate creativity (Boyce-Tillman, 2012). Valuing both the orate *and* literate can enable students to choose their own ways of bringing reason and emotion together.

Autonomy

Self-control—or the right balance of reason and emotion—was central to ancient Greek thinking and included the reflexivity that is essential to Maslow's self-actualization. In Maslow's needs-pyramid this is close to the aesthetic. This capacity is linked with personal empowerment leading to self-esteem and the ability to make self-initiated decisions. Much music education in its concentration on "musical literacy" has led to the demusicalization of many students (Morgan & Boyce-Tillman, 2016). This has been true, for example, of learning to sing, which is about regaining personal power and resilience. But in musicking (Small, 1998) there are still two aesthetics operating:

> The classical perspective emphasizing performance, perfection and virtuosity—the standard or "taproot" aesthetic that has been recognised in music education since its inception in the mid-1800s.
>
> The second is an aesthetic for singing which stresses community building, diversity, group collaboration and relationship.
>
> (Pascale, 2005, p. 166)

Everyday creativity, such as humming and singing, is self-regulatory. These have often been stopped by misplaced music education, whether in the form of examinations or well-meaning school teachers (Morgan & Boyce-Tillman, 2016).

Singing can also empower, in a special way, those who have difficulty in learning. In a school for children with special needs, the head teacher saw music as a real possibility for his pupils. School inspectors critiqued the head teacher for doing too much music and not adhering to the minutiae of the curriculum literacy hour. "But look," he said, singling out three girls: "These have learned to read in two weeks in order to learn the songs they want to sing as a pop group!"

Eleanor Gibson (2018), as part of her Farmington Study, focuses on singing, spiritual, and sensory development, in the context of a school for children with severe learning disabilities by taking her students into a local cathedral to experience the sound of their voices singing sacred syllables. So, in claiming a musical voice, people can claim their autonomy and develop their own power and sense of self.

Music and Values

The domain of "values" is inextricably bound up with virtues and ethics. Classical Greek literature is filled with stories embodying the potential ethical power of music (Godwin, 1987, p. 45) but theorists such as Reimer (1970) have often preferred to see individual works of art dislocated from their social context. However:

> the sounds of music serve as well to *create* those structures, and to create them in a dialectic of perception and action *consistent* with the quintessentially symbolic character of human worlds.
>
> (Shepherd & Wicke, 1997, pp. 138–9)

Philosophers such as Subotnik (1996) and Westerlund (2002, p. 144) attempt to restore these cultural dimensions. For example, a ten-year-old boy reflects on a performance (Boyce-Tillman, 2001) that was not controlled by a single conductor and included a multiplicity of pieces some by the children themselves: "It was like peace on earth. Everyone did their own thing, but it all fitted together." Of the same performance the teachers comment on music's ability to develop community building skills, counterbalancing self-centeredness.

There are many narratives on musicking with declared ethical intention that need including in music curricula, thus widening the view of music education from solipsistic inward subjectivity and individual cognition to shared musical events demanding virtues such as respect, mutuality, and collaboration.

The link with notions of community exists in government documents in the UK with the delivery of the citizenship agenda (Department for Education and Skills 2002), including religious, moral, cultural, personal, social, and health issues. Anthony Storr (1993) saw the creation of community as the main reason for the presence of music in world cultures (p. 23). Reflection in this area could prepare pupils for understanding about the use of music in shopping malls, military parades, and political rallies, comparing its manipulative and transformative possibilities within a culture.

Meaning and Purpose

The establishment of personal and cultural value systems relates to a sense of meaning, purpose, and fulfillment. A concern for justice often involves the empowerment of diverse groups of people who have lost a sense of personal significance. A dominant culture of heteropatriarchy has disempowered many people with hierarchies encompassing economics and cultural roles (CMEPSP, 2009). Musicking can give subjugated groups a sense of purpose.

In the arts, women are being re-empowered by the rediscovery of women composers; but still they often struggle to find a secure place in school and university curricula because of the embeddedness of the Western musical canon of male composers. For example, Ethel Smyth (1858–1954), the composer associated with the suffragettes, turned out strong operas, such as *The Wreckers,* described as unbecoming from the pen of a woman. Her work could find a place in the story of opera with her dramatic portrayal of the sea, which influenced Benjamin Britten's Sea Interludes in *Peter Grimes.* Errolyn Wallen's (born 1958) opera, *Another America: Fire*, shows a black female astronaut preparing for her mission to Mars but trapped by her role as a mother. Her ancestors appear in a dreamlike sequence to support her journey, which eventually she undertakes against well-meaning advice. But changing a tradition:

> [may] involve learning new skills and expanding the meaning of concepts, often "unlearning" what was formerly believed to be true.
>
> (Cohen, 2007, p. 31)

Various projects described in *Queering Freedom* show attempts at "truth seeking" and respecting diversity. *Queering the Space – Community Music Work with LGBTQ Groups* tells how Catherine Pestano (2018) helped participants to negotiate the minefield of modern sexual lexicography and alliances, showing how improvisatory creative practices in community music activities can support the development of autonomy in the wider world. A recent project, begun at the University of Winchester entitled *Voice for the Voiceless*,[3] involved initiating a choir in the women's refuge who created their own song, which they sang to the delight of citizens in the center of Winchester, including such lines as:

> Looking for an open door to free my jailed heart … I have survived through the dark … We'll share the weight, there's so much to show, We'll stand together—we're learning to grow.[4]

Andre de Quadros (2018) describes the dilemmas in the search for justice and right relationship involving controversy around the use of a Muslim song in a US school:

> By extension, whatever "sensitivity" they are trying to promote is also supporting racism. That's pretty untenable. What can this teacher do?
>
> (p. 205)

This contested story with the mismatch between the values of the teacher and the surrounding community shows the cost of supporting meaning and purpose within minority communities. It highlights the area of contest and struggle within the journey to eudaimonia and that happiness is only a temporary virtue. Here the teacher's sense of meaning and purpose require courage and resilience.

Music and Spirituality

Aquinas introduced the idea of contact with the Divine into Aristotelian concepts. In a post-secular society, the word "spirituality" (with or without religion; Boyce-Tillman, 2016a) is closer to how many people see the entry into another way of knowing; a time when body, mind, spirit, and emotions come together. Maslow's (1962) peak experience represents the reintegration of the body (Materials), emotions (Expression), reason/intellect (Construction), and culture (Values). Philosophers such as Catherine Ellis (1985) have brought ethnomusicological insights into relationship with Western classical traditions to offer us insight into the spiritual domain. She distinguishes between three levels of learning, informal, formal and spiritual/visionary, which are acknowledged in aboriginal traditions (p. 200). The musickers—be they composers, performers or listeners—enter a different time/space dimension, leaving everyday reality for "another world," the liminal space of Victor Turner (1969, 1974). This liminal/spiritual space is potentially transformative (Boyce-Tillman, 2009a), yielding personal growth. There is a sense of intimacy and I-Thou awareness (Buber 1970), a feeling of being united with the universe, other beings, and the natural world. It is a way of knowing that is different from every day (propositional) knowing. It is a both/and logic, in which a way of not knowing may appear within a paradox accepted as a harmonious self (Clarke, 2005). Here the "beyond" is present as the whole person or community experiences the reintegrating of themselves. There is increasing interest in this area in music education (Boyce-Tillman, 2017).

Contemplation

Aquinas saw the beatific vision as important. It is often most clearly seen in education in Christian contexts, although in other contexts it is being combined with mindfulness (Estenek, 2006; Palmer, 2010). Julie Shaw (2019) draws on the founder of the Order of the Company of Mary Our Lady (Julia Françoise de Toulouse cited in Soury-Lavergne, 1984), in whose school she works, to see education as formation within an environment that encourages openness and dialogue, positive inter-relationship with others, acceptance of differences, sensitivity with regard to social issues, sympathy, and respect. Shaw describes how the Easter Cantata project encourages this spirit of friendship and collaboration, being an entirely communal enterprise. John Burdett (2019) addresses similar issues in higher education, drawing on van der Merwe and Habron's (2017) conceptual model of spirituality in music education. In his evangelical Christian university, participants concentrate on their relationship with God, which is in contrast to their physical life (as in Aquinas). Spiritual maturity is reflective, vulnerable, balanced, self-aware, courageous, humble, willing to lead, and a looking for God in every situation.

Frank Heuser (2017) coined the term equanimity, associated with composure in the face of difficulties, a concept close to the Greek concept of virtue.

Composers have also pondered music's capacity to contemplate the infinite. John Cage, approaching *Silent Prayer*, writes:

> I determined to give up composition unless I could find a better reason for doing it than communication. I found this answer from Gita Sarabhai, an Indian singer and tabla player: The purpose of music is to sober and quiet the mind, thus making it susceptible to divine influences.
>
> (cited in Kostelanetz, 1993, p. 239)

4 minutes 33 seconds (originally called *Silent Prayer*) was a form of resistance that challenges social norms and diffuses power structures. Cage saw it as a connection with the universe and realignment of the body and mind in a spiritual contemplation. The exploration of silence could be an important part of a music curriculum.

Music and the Ancestors

This access to this liminal space can happen by listening to pieces of music from the past, perhaps linked with the Greek idea of the daimons. Western classical composers can function like the spirits of the ancestors in the spirit possession rituals (Boyce-Tillman, 2008/09), giving hope and companionship:

> I had on Brahms' First Symphony (of which I am especially fond) and was in a state of complete relaxation. However, a chord sounded and at once I was removed from my normal life. My whole physical being dissolved, and I knew that I was, in reality, a spiritual creature who only had semblance of a body. I was, quite obviously, the note of music. Not only that, but I was also the light that shone clear blue just to the left of mental vision.
>
> (Maxwell & Tschudin, 1990, p. 156)

These accounts, often suppressed in post-Enlightenment Western secular musical culture, are resurfacing in post secular societies. If students are allowed to be articulate about such experiences in class, it may enable teachers to help them to evaluate the musical "guides" they are choosing and how helpful or unhelpful they may be.

Music and Wonder

The accounts of this liminal state show how music can take musickers to a place of wonder—an important part of the peak experience. De Botton (2012) argues that we no longer need a set of religious or doctrinal beliefs in a God of any kind. However, he suggests that people in this modern age should not feel embarrassed about re-appropriating, for the secular realm, those "consoling, subtle or just charming" religious rituals that inspire, such as "gratitude, beautiful spaces, pilgrimages and singing" (pp. 32–7), all of which, he says, can nourish the spirit and soul in a place of awe and wonder. In an age when many search for meaning and purpose, this non-demanding aspect of the listening experience offers a place for meaning-making. The Dean Emeritus of Winchester cathedral writes of music:[5]

> You are simply invited to let it [the music] anoint you with its costly perfume. It is a gift. No one is demanding anything first, checking your fitness or looking for the right answers. A door is opened in heaven. It is a moment of Christ-inspired generosity. The kingdom is offered without restriction or condition.
>
> (Atwell, 2019, n/p)

Conclusion

A recent choral piece by Jim Papoulis called *Gnothi Safton* (Know thyself), with its opening lines of *Gnothi safton, eudaimonia* encourages singers to "seek beauty, freedom and justice" and "celebrate virtue, prudence, courage and life." This piece resulted from a conversation with the composer about what children felt was important in life. Connection was made with the larger Greek ideas seen in this chapter. The Greek language was included to show this connection.[6] It is an example of a eudaimonic aim within education.

What this survey of music and eudaimonia shows is that curriculum developments such as the plans for the EBacc in the UK, which exclude music and philosophy/religion, run the risk of obliterating large parts of human experience and enculturating children into a bio-mechanical universe:

> In the usual course, I was sent to school, but possibly my suffering was unusual. The non-civilized in me was sensitive: it had a great thirst for colour, for music, for the movement of life … Our city-built education took no heed of that living fact. It had its luggage-van waiting for branded bales of marketable results.
>
> (Tagore & Elmhirst, 1961, p. 53)

Without philosophy/theology, there is nowhere to ask the fundamental questions about life; without the arts, people will not experience the depth and complexity of human emotional, social, spiritual, and physical experiences with their potential to enable them to reach their full human stature.

Notions of eudaimonia, originating in Greek philosophy, were developed by the medieval theologian Thomas Aquinas to include a notion of spirituality. It has formed the basis of current movements in psychology and assessment scales of wellbeing. Links with musical experiences have been explored by means of a phenomenographic map. This chapter has shown how various aspects of these can be developed in music education in ways that challenge traditional music pedagogy. This means not only in changes in music pedagogy but also the protecting of music education in an age which would seem to concentrate on scientific and technological thinking directly related to the world of work. Wonder, awe, generosity of spirit, and a passion for justice and right relationship may be at risk.

Notes

1. www.ons.gov.uk/peoplepopulationandcommunity/wellbeing/articles/measuresofnationalwellbeingdashboard/2018–09–26
2. The spelling used in the UK documents.
3. Funded by The Winchester Centre for the Arts as Wellbeing.
4. From the song written by the Unity Choir, November 2018.
5. This referred originally to the music of the contemporary British composer, John Tavener.
6. www.youtube.com/watch?v=4AEBaokfwS4

References

Abrams, D. (1996). *The spell of the sensuous*. New York: Pantheon Books.

Ackrill, J. L. (1981). *Aristotle the philosopher*. Oxford: Oxford University Press.

Argyle, M. (1997). *The psychological perspective of religious experience* (2nd Series Occasional Paper 8). University of Wales, Lampeter: Alister Hardy Religious Experience Research Centre.

Aristotle. (1922). *The poetics of Aristotle*. Trans. S.H. Butcher. London: Macmillan and Co.

Atwell, J. (2019 in preparation). Brief reflections on Winchester Cathedral and the music of Sir John Tavener. In J. Boyce-Tillman, A. Forbes, & J. Erricker. (Eds.), *The Spirituality of the Music of John Tavener*. Oxford: Peter Lang.

Bastian, H. G. (2000). *Musik(erziehung) und ihre Wirkung. Eine Langzeitstudie an Berliner Grundschulen*. Mainz: Schott.

Batzoglou, A. (2011). Towards a theatre of psychagogia: An experimental application of the Sesame Approach into psychophysical actor training. PhD diss., Central School of Speech and Drama, University of London.

Boyce-Tillman, J. (1996). A framework for intercultural dialogue in music. In M. Floyd (Ed.), *World Musics in Education*, Farnborough: Scolar Books, pp. 43–94.

Boyce-Tillman, J. (1998). *The call of the ancestors*. London: The Hildegard Press.

Boyce-Tillman, J. (2001). Sounding the sacred: Music as sacred site. In K. Ralls-MacLeod & G. Harvey (Eds.), *Indigenous religious musics* (pp. 136–166). Farnborough: Scolar.

Boyce-Tillman, J. (2008/2009). Contacting the ancestors: Music and healing in two traditions. In Antonella Barbarossa (Ed.), *Magia, Esoterismo e Fantasmi; Raccolta Atti del X Convegno Internazionale di Stidi "Filosofia della Musica a Musica della Filosofia"*, Vibo valentia: Ministero dell'Universita e della Ricerca alta Formazione Artistica e Musicale Conservatorio di Musica "F. Torrefranca" pp. 31–42.

Boyce-Tillman, J. (2007). Music and value in cross-cultural work. In O. Urbain (Ed.), *Music and conflict transformation: Harmonies and dissonances in geopolitics* (pp. 40–52). London: I.B. Tauris.

Boyce-Tillman, J. (2012). Music and the dignity of difference. *Philosophy of Music Education Review, 20*(1), 25–44.

Boyce-Tillman, J. (2013). "And still I wander … A look at Western music education through Greek mythology." *Music Educators Journal, 99*(3), 29–33.

Boyce-Tillman, J. (2016a). *Experiencing music—Restoring the spiritual: Music and wellbeing*. Oxford: Peter Lang.

Boyce-Tillman, J. (2016b). Unchained melody: The rise of orality and therapeutic singing. In G. Welch, D. Howard, & J. Nix (Eds.), *The Oxford handbook of singing* (pp. 935–962). Oxford: Oxford University Press.

Boyce-Tillman, J. (Ed.). (2017). *Spirituality and music education: Perspectives from three continents.* Oxford: Peter Lang.

Boyce-Tillman, J. (2018). *Freedom song: Faith, abuse, music and spirituality: A lived experience of celebration.* Oxford: Peter Lang.

Buber, M. (1970). *I and thou.* (K. Walter, trans.). New York: Charles Scribner's Sons.

Burdett, J. (in press). Incorporating spirituality into a 21st century collegiate music curriculum. In J. Boyce-Tillman, S. Roberts & J. Erricker (Eds.). *Enlivening faith, music, spirituality and Christian Theology,* Oxford: Peter Lang.

Chanda, M. L., & Levitin, D. J. (2013). The neurochemistry of music. *Trends in Cognitive Science,* 17, 180–194.

Choudhury, P. (2011). *Luminous life: A new model of humanistic psychotherapy.* Winter Park, CO: Bauu Press.

Clarke, I. (2005). There is a crack in everything, that's how the light gets in. In C. Chris (Ed.), *Ways of knowing: Science and mysticism today* (pp. 90–102). London: Imprint.

Clift, S., Morrison, I., Coulton, S., Treadwell, P., Page, S., Vella-Burrows, T., & Skingley, A. (2013). *A feasibility study on the health benefits of a participative community singing programme for older people with Chronic Obstructive Pulmonary Disease (COPD).* Canterbury Christ Church University, UK: Sidney De Haan Research Centre for Arts and Health.

Cohen, C. (2007). Music: A universal language? In O. Urbain (Ed.), *Music and conflict transformation: Harmonies and dissonances in geopolitics* (pp. 26–39). London: I. B. Tauris.

Commission for the Measurement of Economic Performance and Social Progress (CMEPSP) (2009).

De Botton, A. (2012). *Religion for atheists: A non-believer's guide to the uses of religion.* London: Hamish Hamilton.

De Quadros, A. (2018). What's a music teacher to do? An exploration of opportunities and obstacles to personhood and music within and towards the Muslim World. In K. Hendricks & J. Boyce-Tillman (Eds.), *Queering freedom: Music, identity and spirituality: Anthology with perspectives from over ten countries* (pp. 203–218). Oxford: Peter.

Department for Education and Skills (2002). *Transforming youth work: Resourcing excellent youth services*. London: Department for Education and Skills/Connexions.

Donato, A. (2007). Contemplation as the end of human nature in aquinas's 'sententia libri ethicorum'. In F. D. Blasi, J. P. Hochschild & J. Langan (Eds.), *Virtue's end: God in the moral philosophy of Aristotle and Aquinas* (pp. 27–43). South Bend, IN: St. Augustine's Press.

Dowd, O. (2019). The intersection of spirituality and the ethic of care in music and music education. In J. Boyce-Tillman, R. Stephen & J. Erricker (Eds.), *Enlivening faith, music, spirituality and Christian theology*. Oxford: Peter Lang.

Ellis, C. J. (1985). *Aboriginal music: Education for living*. Queensland: University of Queensland Press.

Estenek, S. M. (2006). Redefining spirituality: A new discourse. *College Student Journal, 40*(2), 270–281.

Gibson, E. (2018). *1,2,3 Aaaaaah!* Paper presented at the Tavener International Study Day, University of Winchester, UK.

Girdzijauskas, A. (2017). Different signs of spirituality following different types of music education. In J. Boyce-Tillman (Ed.), *Spirituality and music education: Perspectives from three continents* (pp. 259–278). Oxford: Peter Lang.

Godwin, J. (1987). *Music, magic and mysticism: A sourcebook*. London: Arkana.

Green, L. (1988). *Music on deaf ears: Musical meaning, ideology and education*. Manchester: Manchester University Press.

Green, L. (1997). *Music, gender, education*. Cambridge: Cambridge University Press.

Heuser, F. (2017). Music education and spirituality: Ethical concerns and responsibilities from a U.S. perspective. In J. Boyce-Tillman (Ed.), *Spirituality and music education: Perspectives from three continents* (pp. 103–120). Oxford: Peter Lang.

Kemp, A. E. (1996). *The musical temperament*. Oxford: Oxford University Press.

Kostelanetz, R. (2003). *Conversing with Cage*. New York: Routledge.

Kung, H. (1992). *Mozart: Traces of transcendence*. London: SCM.

Marton, F., & Booth, S. (1997). *Learning and awareness*. Mahwah NJ: Lawrence Erlbaum Associates.

Maslow, A. H. (1962). Toward a psychology of being. Princeton: D. Van Nostrand Company.

Maslow, A. H. (1970a). *Motivation and personality*. New York: Harper & Row.

Maslow, A. H. (1970b). *Religions, values, and peak experiences*. New York: Penguin. (Original work published 1966).

Maslow A.H. (1971). *The farther reaches of human nature*, New York, NY: Viking.

Maxwell, M., & Tschudin, V. (2005). *Seeing the invisible: Modern religious and other transcendent experiences*. Lampeter, Wales: Religious Experience Research Centre, University of Wales.

Miller, A. (1987). *For your own good—The roots of violence in child-rearing*. London: Virago.

Morgan, S., & Boyce-Tillman, J. (2016). *A river rather than a road: The community choir as spiritual experience*. Oxford: Peter Lang.

Morrison, I., & Clift, S. (2012). Singing and mental health. Canterbury: Canterbury Christchurch University.

Noddings, N. (1984). *Caring, a feminine approach to ethics and moral education.* Berkeley, CA: University of California Press.

Noddings, N. (1992). *The challenge to care in school: an alternative approach to education,* New York: Teachers College Press.

Noddings, N. (2002). *Starting at home: Caring and social policy.* Berkeley, CA: University of California Press.

Palmer, A. J. (2010). Spirituality in music education: Transcending culture, exploration III. *Philosophy of Music Education Review, 18*(2), 152–170.

Pascale, L. M. (2005). Dispelling the myth of the non-singer: Embracing two aesthetics for singing. *Philosophy of Music Education Review, 13*, 165–175.

Pestano, C. (2018). Queering the space: Community music work with LGBTQ groups. In K. Hendricks & J. Boyce-Tillman (Eds.), *Queering freedom: Music, identity and spirituality—Anthology with perspectives from over ten countries* (pp. 151–168). Oxford: Peter Lang.

Piliciauskas, A. (1998). *Muzikos pažinimas (Musical Cognition).* Vilnius: LAMUC.

Rahn, J. (1994). What is valuable in art, and can music still achieve it? In J. Rahn (Ed.), *Perspectives in musical aesthetics* (pp. 54–65). New York: Norton.

Reimer, B. (1970). *A philosophy of music education.* Englewood Cliffs, NJ: Prentice Hall.

Rogers, C. (1976). *On becoming a person.* London: Constable.

Ryff, C. D. (1989). Happiness is everything, or is it? Explorations on the meaning of psychological well-being. *Journal of Personality and Social Psychology, 57*(6), 1069–1081.

Seligman, M. (2011). *Flourish: A visionary new understanding of happiness and well-being.* New York: Free Press.

Seligman, M., & Csikszentmihalyi, M. (2000). Positive psychology: An introduction. *American Psychologist. 55*(1), 5–14.

Shaw, J. (in press). The road to Emmaus: An easter cantata. In J. Boyce-Tillman, S. Roberts & J. Erricker (Eds.), *Enlivening faith, music, spirituality and Christian theology.* Oxford: Peter Lang.

Shepherd, J., & Wicke, P. (1997). *Music and cultural theory.* Cambridge: Polity Press.

Simon, P. (1994). Graceland. In White, Timothy *Lasers in the jungle: The conception and maturity of a musical masterpiece* CD 9 46430–2 Warner Brothers.

Soury-Lavergne, F. (1984). *A pathway in education.* Rome, Italy: Imprimi Potest.

Small, C. (1998). *Musicking: The meanings of performing and listening.* London: Wesleyan University Press.

Storr, A. (1993). *Music and the mind.* London: HarperCollins.

Subotnik, R. R. (1996). *Deconstructive variations: Music and reason in Western society.* Minneapolis, MN: University of Minnesota Press.

Tagore, R., & Elmhirst, L.K. (1961). *Rabindranath Tagore. Pioneer in education. Essays and exchanges between Rabindranath Tagore and L.K. Elmhirst.* London: John Murray.

Turner, V. (1969/1974). *The ritual process: Structure and anti-structure.* Baltimore, MD: Penguin Books.

Urbain, O. (Ed.). (2007). *Music and conflict transformation: Harmonies and dissonances in geopolitics.* London: I.B. Tauris.

van der Merwe, L., & Habron, J. (2017). A conceptual model of spirituality in music education. In J. Boyce-Tillman (Ed.), *Spirituality and music education: Perspectives from three continents* (pp. 19–48). Oxford: Peter Lang.

Walker, J., & Boyce-Tillman, J. (2002). Music lessons on prescription? The impact of music lessons for children with chronic anxiety problems. *Health Education—The Arts and Health*, *102*(4), pp. 172–179.

Westerlund, H. (2002). *Bridging experience, action, and culture in music education.* Studia Musica 16, Helsinki: Sibelius Academy.

Williams R. (2017). Lecture at Holy Rood House, July.

Winner, E., & Hetland, L. (2000). *Beyond the soundbite: Arts education and academic outcomes.* Los Angeles, CA: The Getty Center.

Witkin, R. (1974). *The intelligence of feeling*. London: Heinemann.

8 Listening and the Happiness of the Musician

Sophie Haroutunian-Gordon and Megan Jane Laverty

How can making music *well* contribute to the happiness (*eudaimonia*) of the musician? In what follows, we offer an argument for the following claim: listening and meaning making contribute to making music well and are necessary for the happiness of the musician. The argument proceeds through the following four steps. First, we define "eudaimonia" according to Aristotle: human beings achieve "happiness" over a lifetime if they "act" consistently with the "rational principle" and achieve "excellence" and "pleasure" by so doing. The words in quotation are technical terms for which Aristotle gives specific definitions in his *Nicomachean Ethics.* Step One of our argument involves presenting Aristotle's definitions of the terms and thereby, explaining what he means by "happiness."

Having clarified Aristotle's conception of happiness, Step Two is to characterize the happiness of a musician. We do this by means of a specific example in which an experienced piano student, Sophie, is learning to play Franz Schubert's *Moments Musicaux Number One* (see Figures 8.1a and 8.1b), with the help of her teacher, Deborah Sobol. The reader is introduced to the student, the teacher, and the piece of music under consideration.

In Step Three, we begin to argue that in learning to play Schubert's piece well, both student and teacher are involved in "listening" as the contemporary philosopher, Jean-Luc Nancy (2002/2007) defines that term. Nancy maintains that listening is striving to make meaning out of sounds that one encounters. We then present Nancy's account of listening in some detail.

In Step Four, we show the student and teacher working to make meaning of the music as played and the things that they say to one another. The meaning that the student makes seems to help her to play the piece better, thus moving her toward what Aristotle has in mind by "excellence." The meaning that the teacher makes contributes to the student's progress. Thus, the lesson brings with it apparent occasions of what Aristotle calls "pleasure" for both participants. Such occasions, we maintain, contribute to the happiness of the musician.

Step One: Aristotle's Conception of *Eudaimonia*

Eudaimonia, according to Aristotle, is human happiness (1097b, p. 22).[1] Human happiness is, he writes, "something complete … and is the end of action" (1997b, p. 20). It is complete in the sense that happiness is sought for its own sake and not for the sake of something else (1097a, pp. 25–28). Happiness is the chief good for which everything else is done (1097b, pp. 5–7).

Furthermore, human beings undertake actions for reasons. Their reasons for acting have to do with the perceived value of what they do, or what they are aiming at by way of what they do. In other words, individuals perform actions for reasons that are directly related to the activity itself, or they perform actions that they think will lead to, or culminate in, other valued outcomes. Aristotle writes: "Since there are [sic] evidently more than one end, and we choose some of these (e.g., wealth, flutes, and in general instruments) for the sake of something else, clearly not all ends are complete ends; but the chief good is evidently something complete" (1097a, pp. 25–28). Here, he explicitly states that flute playing, or the playing of musical instruments, is pursued "for the sake of something else" (ibid). In other words, while making music is not a complete end, for the musician it is a means to the complete end, namely happiness.

Aristotle goes on to argue that "happiness … comes as a result of excellence" (1099b, p. 15) or, more specifically, human excellence. Human excellence is "an activity of the soul (*psyche*)" (1102a, pp. 14–17). Our souls make possible our engagement in excellent activity. Excellent activity accords with the "rational principle" (1098a, pp. 7–8). To act according to the rational principle is to choose goals, to choose steps to meet those goals, and to successfully execute those steps. Excellence involves performing actions well. To say that an action is performed well is to say that it has achieved the standard of excellence.

Pleasure can arise from performing the action well. For Aristotle, pleasure is a state of the soul (1099a, p. 5)—a byproduct of activity. It results from the pursuit of what one loves or is most passionate about (1099a, pp. 5–6). In other words, pleasure occurs when a person is engaged in what he or she loves to do. If a person loves performing certain actions well, then that person is going to discover that "[those] excellent actions must be in themselves pleasant" (1099a, p. 21).

In summary, Aristotle argues that happiness is something complete and the end of all action. All actions aim at some good, and the most complete good is happiness. To act according to the rational principle is to choose goals, identify the steps needed to achieve those goals, and successfully execute those steps. To achieve such excellence in the pursuit of one's goals brings pleasure. Thus, pleasure accompanies the activities done well and those activities bring about happiness. In the next section, we move on to a discussion of our example, relating Aristotle's conception of happiness to the happiness of the musician.

Step Two: The Happiness of a Musician

Given Aristotle's conception of happiness, we now argue that making music, at least the performance of Western classical music, is an activity of the soul in accordance with the rational principle. Furthermore, such music-making, if done well, is accompanied by pleasure for the musician and contributes to the happiness of which Aristotle speaks. To make the argument, we present an excerpt from a dialogue between an adult piano student, Sophie, and her teacher, Deborah. The lesson in which the dialogue took place occurred on November 15, 2007. It focused on Franz Schubert's *Sechs (Six) Moments Musicaux,* Op. 94–D.780. Deborah, sadly deceased 2014, was a well-known pianist and chamber musician who had studied in Vienna—Schubert's birthplace and home. Indeed, her experience finds its way into the lesson, which concerned the first of the six *Moment Musicaux.*[2]

Picture the teacher and her student seated at two different pianos positioned side by side. The teacher says:

1. *Deborah*: Now, do this for me if you would (plays measures 27–29) and let's talk about this.
2. next transition.
3. *Sophie*: (plays measures 27–29)
4. *Deborah*: Beautiful. Now, while that's holding [the sound from measure 29]—
5. *Sophie*: (plays measures 30–37)
6. *Deborah*: Let's repeat, Sophie.
7. *Sophie*: (plays the same measures; Deborah sings along)

In Aristotle's terms, one might say that playing these measures is an activity of the human soul: it involves action that is guided by the rational principle, for the player follows a series of steps in order to render, on the piano, the notes and other marks printed on the page.

The transcript gives evidence that as Sophie plays measures 27–37, and as Deborah responds to her playing, they act as they do to reach goals. When Deborah begins by asking Sophie to play measures 27–29 (lines 1–2) and says, "let's talk about this next transition," she indicates that she has a goal in mind, namely to make possible a discussion of the movement from measure 29 to 30 ("transition"). We see that Sophie complies with the request (line 3). The goal of her action—her playing of measures 27–29—is to provide an audible rendition of the music in the printed score and thereby, do as Deborah requests. The actions of both student and teacher are consistent with the goals that they have and are undertaken to achieve those goals.

Let us underscore the point that the goals of both student and teacher are musicians' goals, and the actions that each undertakes to meet the goals are musicians' actions. We define a "musician" as someone who wants to make music and who does, or tries to do, things that will achieve the goal of making music—in the present case, rendering the music of Schubert's *Moment Musicaux* No. 1 on the piano. The actions thus far observed are activities of the soul in accordance with the rational principle because they indicate the goals—the musical goals—and the actions chosen and executed in order to meet them.

After Sophie repeats measures 30–37, her teacher says:

8. *Deborah*: You played that so beautifully, Sophie. Now, take us some place else—
9. *Sophie*: (begins to play measure 38)
10. *Deborah*: OK, hang on a second.
11. *Sophie*: (stops playing)
12. *Deborah*: All of this is about atmosphere painting, each one of these sections—this is why I
13. love this music so much. It's all about sound atmosphere. (Deborah plays measures 38–39,
14. the transition between two sections)—We're in a whole different place now, right? So let's
15. do that now. I love the way you played [measures 30–37]: I feel like I'm in a shepherd's
16. hut (laughs), listening to a little song. It's so intimate all of a sudden [at measure 38]. Just
17. play that measure [38] for me.

In line 8, we have evidence that Sophie not only identified a goal and executed actions to reach it but, according to the teacher, executed the actions well. When she says, "You played that so beautifully, Sophie," she seems to mean that Sophie's playing of measures 27–37 achieved such standards of excellence as she, the teacher, held. Deborah seems to take pleasure in music well played—much as musicians should do. Perhaps the student also felt pleasure in playing the measures well, although the transcript does not tell us that.

However, the teacher's pleasure seems to have been interrupted. For as Sophie begins to play measure 38 (line 9), Deborah says, "OK, hang on a second" (line 10). In lines 12 through 15, she tells us why she stopped Sophie's playing: 1) the music is "about atmosphere painting," meaning perhaps: playing these measures should create a certain "sound atmosphere," a certain feeling or sensation in the listener; 2) the sound atmosphere to be created by the playing of measure 38 is to be different from that created by the playing of measures 27–37: "We're in a whole different place now, right? So let's do that now." Evidently, while Deborah experienced pleasure listening to Sophie play measures 27–37, she is taken aback as Sophie begins playing measure 38: "It's so intimate all of a sudden" (line 16). When Deborah says, "Play that measure for me" (line 17), she directs the student to create a feeling of closeness ("intimacy") beginning measure 38.

18. *Sophie*: (plays measures 38–41)
19. *Deborah*: Watch those accents [measure 42].
20. *Sophie*: (plays measures 42–44, while Deborah plays along with her)
21. *Deborah*: Bravo, Sophie. You hardly ever hear it that way.

Note that the accents are on beats one and three in measure 42 and on beat 2 in measure 43. Evidently, the teacher plays along with Sophie to let her experience the sound of the accented notes that she should want to hear in playing those measures. When she says, "Bravo Sophie, you hardly ever hear it that way," it is not clear whether she is cheering the student's performance of measures 42 through 44 (Could she hear it if she was playing along?) or the sound of the accented notes, played as they are marked in the score.

22. *Deborah*: You see this, this is seminal. Back in measures 6 and 7, those three big beats [Note the accents on beats one and three, measure 6, and beat two, measure 7].

Deborah's point is that the pattern of accents appearing in measures 6 and 7 also appear in measures 42 and 43. In drawing Sophie's attention to the re-emergence of that pattern, Deborah shows her student that playing well involves seeing what the composer put in the score and rendering it. Omitting the accents marked in measure 42, as Deborah seems to fear Sophie may do (see line 19) defeats the musician's goal of playing Schubert's music well. And hearing the way Sophie played measure 38 (line 10) seems to move Deborah not only to point out the notation in measure 42 and 43 and play it, but in addition, to show the student why the accents must be observed: they appear in the score as a pattern not once but twice, indicating that Schubert thinks the pattern is important enough to be sounded again. The pattern is "seminal" Deborah declares (line 22).

The lesson continues:

32. *Deborah*: Also, sorry, one more thing (plays measures 38–43). Because it's moderato, this dotted rhythm—[see. e.g., measure 38, beat 2, measure 39, beat 1, also measures 40, 41]—

33. you can assimilate this to the triplet, because the rule is: if it's pianissimo and it's slower,
34. singing, you can do that.
35. *Sophie*: Yes, that's what I was trying to do.
36. *Deborah*: It's a little sharp, which makes it harder to sing that way.
37. *Sophie*: (plays measure 37 again)
38. *Deborah*: No, see even there—sing the triplet underneath it.
39. *Sophie*: (plays measure 37 again)
40. *Deborah*: Beautiful.
41. *Sophie*: (continues playing measures 38, 39, 40, 41, 42, 43, 44) [four of the measures continue the dotted rhythm]
42. *Deborah*: Bravo, Sophie.

Again, Deborah draws Sophie's attention to the standards of excellence that she holds, this time in reference to playing of the dotted rhythms in measures 38–41: "You can assimilate them to the triplet," meaning: you can play the sixteenth notes in the score with a note of a triplet figure, not before or after it. Sophie says that she was "trying to do that" [line 37], but the teacher says, "It's a little sharp," meaning that the sixteenth note did not sound simultaneously with a note of the triplet figure. To help her student, Deborah suggests, "sing the triplet underneath it" [line 38], that is: play the melody line while you sing the triplet rhythm so that you sound the sixteenth note in the score at the same time you sing one note in the triplet. Deborah's comment at line 42 indicates that Sophie succeeded in playing the dotted rhythm as directed. In so doing, Sophie achieves another "moment of excellence"—a moment where she reaches the high standards Deborah has set. Apparently, Sophie's playing brings pleasure to her teacher [line 42] and perhaps to herself, although again, the transcript does not tell us that.

Looking at the previous example, we have evidence that Deborah, an accomplished musician and teacher, is on the path of what Aristotle calls happiness—the happiness of a musician. At some moments, she expresses pleasure when she hears Sophie play well [e.g., lines 4, 8, 15, 21, 41]. At the same time, when her pleasure is interrupted [e.g., lines 10, 32], she identifies goals of excellence that she believes the student should strive to meet, at times specifying actions Sophie can take to meet the goals. Sophie, an aspiring musician, seems to embrace the standards of excellence that Deborah offers, as she responds so as to meet them. Perhaps she, too, in meeting them at moments, experiences pleasure in so doing.

As we have seen, making music well, and achieving moments of pleasure, and perhaps a lifetime of happiness as a musician, as Deborah may have done, requires not only musical standards of excellence, but also the ability to meet them. Further analysis of our example reveals that in order to help Sophie play well, Deborah must engage in listening to her student play.

In what follows, we present a definition of "listening" offered by Jean-Luc Nancy and using Nancy's framework, describe how Deborah's, and to a lesser extent Sophie's, listening proceeds. We argue that by listening as she does, the teacher helps her student to play well, at least at moments, and thus move herself and Sophie toward the happiness that musicians can enjoy.

Step Three: Jean-Luc Nancy's Conception of Listening

To say that someone has been listening is to say that there is evidence of just that. So, what do we mean by "listening"? Here we turn to Jean-Luc Nancy's *À l'écoute* for a useful definition of listening (2002, 2007).[3] The value of Nancy's conception is that it presents a formal structure of listening. Accordingly, listening has the same characteristics no matter the context: an infant listening to the sound of footsteps coming down the hallway, a traffic guard listening to the sound of what might be a train whistle or a musician listening to the performance of Schubert's *Moments Musicaux No. One*. In all cases, "to listen is to be straining toward a possible meaning, and consequently one that is not immediately accessible (Nancy, 2007, p. 6)". Put differently, to listen is to be "on the edge of meaning" (Nancy, 2007, p. 7). Nancy uses the term "listening" to refer to the effort to make meaning/sense (Fr. *sens*) of sounds. He contrasts "listening" with "hearing" when he says that to "hear" is to have made meaning/sense —to believe oneself to have understood (as cited in Nancy, 2002, pp. 16–18; 2007, p. 6). Listening, on the other hand, refers to the process of making sense of what one hears—of coming to an idea of what one has heard.

How does the listener make meaning/sense of a sound(s)—to conclude that a shrill whining sound is made by a train whistle rather than a bird, for example? Nancy (2007) writes:

> One can say, then, at least, that meaning and sound share the space of a referral, in which at the same time they refer to each other, and that, in a very general way, this space can be defined as the space of a *self*, a subject. A *self* is nothing other than a form or function of referral: a *self* is made of a relationship *to* self, or of a presence *to* self, which is nothing other than the mutual referral between a perceptible individuation and an intelligible identity (not just the individual in the current sense of the word, but in him the singular occurrences of a state, a tension, or, precisely, a "sense") … and the point or occurrence of a *subject* in the substantial sense would have never taken place except in the referral, thus in spacing and resonance … the repetition where the sound is amplified and spreads, as well as the turning back (*rebroussement*) [is] where the echo is made by making itself heard. … A subject *feels*; that is his characteristic and his definition. … When one is listening, one is on the lookout for a subject, something (itself) that identifies *itself* by resonating from

> self to self … and the echo is like the very sound of its sense. But the sound of sense is how it refers to *itself* or how it sends back to itself [*s'envoie*] or *addresses itself*, and thus how it makes sense.
>
> (pp. 8–9; emphasis in original)

Here, Nancy seems to assert that sense making occurs through the mutual referral [Fr. *renvoi*] between the "perceptible individuation" and "an intelligible identity." We interpret the "perceptible individuation" to be an instance of sound(s) encountered by a listener at some moment(s). An "intelligible identity" refers to the listener's constellation of meanings, some of which, perhaps many of which, are related to the sound(s). In listening, the "subject" is the meaning that is created by returning or going back [*renovi*] to this constellation of meanings in an effort to make sense of the sound that the listener encounters. The subject is a felt meaning, a recognition of sameness—an echo—between the instance of sound and one or more meanings in a listener's constellation. That recognition is felt in the "space of a referral." Each meaning is what Nancy calls a "self," and it is a meaning that is formed as a result of relating meanings. Thus, the subject is formed through feeling the "resonating from self to self," that is, the "perceptible individuation" and the "intelligible identity," or aspects of it, echoing one another. The subject feels the resonating and the listener strains to make sense of the feeling resonating.

In our example, Deborah and Sophie listen to Sophie's playing of Schubert's first of the *Sechs Moments Musicaux.* At times, the meaning of what they hear is different for each, as Deborah's "intelligible identity"—the constellation of meanings that she brings to Sophie's performance—exceeds that of the student's. For Deborah, an accomplished pianist, has knowledge of Schubert's music that goes way beyond the work at hand. She has studied it and other works by the composer with a teacher in Vienna as part of her graduate school training. Indeed, she spent many hours copying her teacher's fingerings from his scores so as to realize the music as he might have done. We watch as Deborah strains to make meaning of the sounds she hears as Sophie plays, referring them to such things as the musical standards she has acquired, the musical score itself, and the long history of personal associations that have accrued. Deborah then uses her listening to teach Sophie what she herself should want to hear if she is going to play the music well.

Step Four: Deborah and Sophie's Listening

In what follows, we look for places where Deborah and/or Sophie try to make meaning of the words and sounds that they encounter. Furthermore, we look for evidence of the meaning that each seems to have made. So, let us turn to the seven places in the transcript to see what Sophie and Deborah are doing when they listen.

Listening: The First Place

Line 4 in the transcript is the first time that we see evidence that Deborah has been listening. She says the word "beautiful" after Sophie plays measures 27–29. She makes a judgment about the quality of the sound. But has she listened according to Nancy's conception of listening? Has she tried to make meaning out of the sounds she has encountered, experiencing tension as she related them to the indications in the score, her musical standards, and other elements in the constellation of meanings she brings to auditory experience? She declares the playing was "beautiful," which we interpret to mean that she is satisfied with Sophie's playing of those measures—her standards have been met. But do we see her on "the edge of meaning," that is, struggling to make sense of what she hears?

After the word "beautiful," Deborah says, "Now, while that's holding," meaning: while the sound of measure 29 is sustained so that we continue to hear it. Her comment ends as Sophie plays measures 30–37. Here is the first evidence of struggle—of Deborah's listening, of striving to make meaning, to hear something, perhaps about the nature of the relation between Sophie's conception of the connection between measure 29 and the measures immediately following it. What is it that Deborah is struggling to hear?

Listening: The Second Place

Line 6 in the transcript is the second time we have textual evidence that Deborah has been listening to Sophie play, for she asks Sophie to "repeat." We do not know why Deborah asked for repetition of the measures. She may have wanted to hear them played a second time or she may have wanted Sophie to hear them again. However, we know from lines 1–2 that Deborah is intending to talk with Sophie about transitions—about what happens when the pianist finishes playing one section and begins playing the next. Maybe when she says, "Let's repeat," she means: play again measures 27–29, followed by measures 30–37. She may ask for the repetition because she is not sure whether she heard the transition from 29 to 30 as she wants it. Sophie may not be thinking of measure 30 as a transition measure, or realize that Deborah wants to hear the transition. In short, Deborah may be struggling to hear whether Sophie has given thought to the transition in measure 30 which Deborah seeks to hear there.

Listening: The Third Place

At Line 8, Deborah says "You played that so beautifully, Sophie," referring to the rendition of measures 30–37 that Sophie has just offered. Here, as in Line 4, Deborah makes a judgment about the sounds that she just heard, apparently satisfied with the quality of Sophie's playing of these measures. It seems that once again the teacher's standards have been met. But, despite her approbation, Deborah's focus appears to be elsewhere, for she continues on line 8 saying, "Now take us someplace else." This time, there is no doubt about what Deborah wants to hear: a difference in sound between measures 30–37 and measure 38. Does she hear the sound she is seeking?

Listening: The Fourth Place

At line 9, Sophie begins to play measure 38. At line 10, Deborah interrupts Sophie's playing of measure 38. Although we cannot know precisely what Deborah is thinking, it seems likely that the sounds she hears indicate that Sophie has not understood the instruction. For the sounds Sophie produces on the piano do not "take us someplace else," at least as far as Deborah is concerned. For this reason, perhaps, Deborah goes on to explain to Sophie what she is looking for when she asks her to "take us someplace else."

At lines 8 and 9, there is little question that Deborah is listening: she is struggling to determine whether the sounds that Sophie produces when playing measure 38 will be different in character from those of the previous measures—whether they will arouse different feelings in the listener. As the student begins to play measure 38, the teacher's question is resolved: the answer is no. As the lesson continues, we glimpse the "intelligible identity" —the constellation of meanings that Deborah has brought to bear in listening to Sophie play measure 38. We see the meanings, the "selfs," as Nancy calls them, that send her striving for resoundings, for echoes, that she does not hear as Sophie plays measure 38.

Listening: The Fifth Place

Lines 12–17 provide evidence of what Deborah is doing when she listens to Sophie play. In lines 12–13, she says, "All of this is about atmosphere painting" and "It's all about sound atmosphere." In so saying, Deborah refers to her "intelligible identity"—her conception of what Schubert is doing with the music. She says that he intends to create atmospheres, meaning perhaps feelings of a time and place. Deborah thereby indicates that the pianist's goal is to create sound vivid enough to draw the listener into feeling that time and place. The association to "sound atmosphere painting" is a meaning in the constellation that Deborah brings to her listening of Sophie's performance, and she struggles to hear what the student is doing (or not doing) to reach that goal.

In lines 13–14, we see Deborah playing measures 38–39, and she says, "We're in a whole different place now, right?" She seems to ask Sophie whether she has heard a difference between the "sound atmosphere" of measures 38–39 and the one created by measures 30–37. In playing measures 38 and 39, Deborah shows Sophie how she thinks these measures should sound, that is, what playing these measures well means to her. Here, Deborah's struggle to make meaning out of Schubert's music and out of what she hopes Sophie will hear in it is informed by the score—another in the constellation of meanings that Deborah brings to her listening of Sophie's performance. For measure 38 begins with an accented (>) pianissimo ("pp") on the first beat. Those dynamic markings, as well as others on the page, help to set Deborah's expectation of what she hopes to hear in Sophie's playing of the measure.

In lines 14–15, and in line 17, Deborah asks Sophie to again play measure 38, apparently hoping to hear a change from the atmosphere created by her playing of measures 30–37. Once more, the teacher draws from her constellation of meanings, her "intelligible identity," to help Sophie grasp the nature of the sound she should produce in playing measure 38. To begin, Deborah refers to her idea of the sound Sophie created when playing measures 30–37, which Deborah says she "loves" (line 15). Next, she refers to the way she felt in listening to that sound—"like I'm in a shepherd's hut (laughs) listening to a little song." Here we see Deborah making meaning of something she felt—of grasping a feeling and identifying what Nancy calls a "subject"—a meaning or idea which describes a feeling that she then conveys to Sophie. What she hears seems to echo the experience of being in shepherd's hut and listening to a little song perhaps played on a pipe—an experience she may have had while studying in Vienna. Finally, in line 16, she seems to refer to the dynamic markings that Schubert has placed in measure 38 and declares, "It's so intimate all of a sudden." The accented pianissimo she sees on the first beat of the measure seems to refer Deborah back to the feeling of closeness—of "intimacy." That feeling, she declares, should be aroused in the listener by the playing of measure 38. That feeling is the new meaning that needs to be created in playing the measure.

Now, by talking about measure 38 with reference to the atmosphere of a little shepherd's hut that is created by Sophie's playing of measures 30 to 37, Deborah is working to expand and refine Sophie's "intelligible identity" i.e. the set of meanings that she, Sophie, can refer to when she hears the playing of measure 38. If Deborah can reconfigure Sophie's "intelligible identity," then she can make it possible for Sophie to hear the playing of measure 38 according to how it should be played. Sophie will strain to hear in the playing of measure 38 a meaning that she had not looked for prior to her music lesson with Deborah. Keeping what Deborah has said in mind, Sophie will play measure 38 with the view to creating a "perceptible individuation" that resonates with the "perceptible individuation" that Deborah created when she played measure 38. By talking with Sophie about what she hears and wants to hear, Deborah is contributing to the building of new meanings and "selfs."

Listening: The Sixth Place

At line 18, Sophie plays measures 38–41. At line 19, Deborah seems to be focused on the score when she says, "Watch those accents," referring to the accents that are coming up on beats one and three in measure 42 and beat two in measure 43. Perhaps Deborah fears that she will not hear those beats accented as she wishes to hear them—as she would hear them if the measures were well played. Here, the teacher refers back to what she thinks she should hear, given her idea of how the measures should sound. Indeed, she seems so eager to hear the accents on those bars properly played that she plays measures 42 and 43 along with Sophie (line 20).

On line 21, Deborah says "Bravo Sophie. You hardly ever hear it that way." But here we must ask: Was the teacher listening to the student? Could she have been trying to make meaning of the sound produced by the student if she was playing along with her? When Deborah says "Bravo, Sophie," she may mean that the sound created at line 20—created by both of them—was the sound one should seek to make. Perhaps Deborah was referring the sound she heard as they both played—"the perceptible individuation"—to ideas in her constellation of meanings, such as the meanings of certain dynamic markings. As she felt the resonance between what she believed she should hear and the sound that she perceived, she cheered.

The possibility that at line 21, Deborah was listening to the sound produced rather than the student's performance gains credence as she adds, "You hardly ever hear it that way," meaning: people often don't play the accents as they should, and as you just heard them played. The comment suggests that Deborah was struggling to hear the desired sound rather than what the student was playing. Thus, she played along to show Sophie what she should strive to hear.

Again, at line 22, when Deborah says, "You see this is seminal. Back in measures 6–7 those three big beats," she hears the same pattern of accents repeated in measures 42–43. The importance of pattern of accents in the latter instance is increased, Deborah seems to say, by the fact of its being a repetition. So, Sophie had better play the pattern as written if she wants to play Schubert's piece well.

From here, Deborah is going to talk about how to play a dotted rhythm.

Listening: The Seventh Place

In lines 32–42, Deborah is looking to hear the dotted rhythm rendered in a particular way. Her assessment of Sophie's playing (line 36) is that it is too "sharp." Deborah asks Sophie to play the dotted rhythm again, hoping that she will alter her playing accordingly. Sophie complies, beginning with measure 37. But in Deborah's assessment the desired sound is still missing.

To help Sophie, Deborah introduces a further instruction, which proves efficacious. That Sophie is eventually able to play the dotted rhythm correctly indicates that she has been listening. Furthermore, her playing of the rhythm each time provides evidence of the meaning that she makes while listening to Deborah's words and the sounds she herself produces as she depresses the keys. Let us now look more closely at their conversation.

At lines 32–34, Deborah seeks to improve Sophie's playing of measures 38–43 by asking her to "assimilate" the dotted rhythm to the triplet figure—to play the dotted rhythm as if she were playing it with a note of a three-note figure in which each of the notes is played evenly. At line 35, Sophie says, "Yes, that's what I was trying to do." Yet, at line 38, we see that Sophie has not succeeded, as Deborah says, "No, see even there," meaning that even Sophie's attempt to play measure 37, which has a dotted rhythm in it, has not produced the desired sound (see line 37). It appears that Sophie has not yet made a meaning of Deborah's words that allows her to produce the sound the teacher seeks to hear.

To help Sophie produce the desired sound of the dotted rhythm, Deborah adds (line 38): "sing the triplet underneath it." The transcript does not indicate that Sophie then sings a triplet figure aloud. But, at line 39, she plays measure 37 yet again, and Deborah says, "Beautiful." The teacher's comment indicates that Sophie may have counted the triplet numerals (1, 2, 3) evenly in her head and played the 16th note of the dotted figure correctly, that is, with the third note of the triplet. At line 41 of the transcript, we see that Sophie plays measures 38–44, four of which contain the dotted rhythm (viz. measures 38, 39, 40 and 41). When, Deborah says, "Bravo, Sophie," (line 42), there is evidence that Sophie has now heard and produced the sound of the dotted rhythm that Deborah was seeking to hear—not just once but several times.

Looking even more closely at the dialogue about measures 32–42, we see evidence of the meanings that both teacher and student make as they listen. When in line 35, Sophie says, "Yes, that's what I was trying to do," she gives evidence that she believes that she grasped and has already attempted to do what Deborah has suggested. When Deborah says "it is a little sharp … " (line 36), after which Sophie plays measure 37 again (line 37), followed by Deborah's comment "No, see even there—sing the triplet underneath it," we have evidence that the teacher determines she must tell the student what to do to produce the desired sound. That is the meaning Deborah makes of Sophie's failures seen at lines 35 and 37. Indeed, the meaning Sophie makes of Deborah's instruction allows the student to hear the desired sound—a dotted rhythm that was not "sharp"—and to produce it not once but several times. In addition, the pattern in the musical score indicating the dotted rhythm has assumed a new meaning for Sophie: she can now associate it with the triplet figure when rendering it—a practice that will be useful in many circumstances.

Conclusion

Having completed our examination of an example in which an experienced piano student, Sophie, studies measures in the first of Schubert's *Moments Musicaux* with her teacher, Deborah, we are now ready to return to our original question: How can making music *well* contribute to the happiness of the musician? Let us begin by recalling the results of our analysis. Making music well involves listening. Listening, as Nancy defines it, involves making meaning. To make meaning of the sound(s) that she encounters ("perceptible individuation"), the listener refers back to the meanings she associates with the sound(s) (her "intelligible identity"). In making the association, what Nancy calls a "subject" is created—an echo between the sound(s) encountered and the meanings that it calls up. The listener strives to make sense of the echo that has been felt and in so doing may arrive at new meaning. As we have seen from the example, the discovery of new meaning allows the musician to make music better and to move toward the goal of making music well.

Furthermore, our analysis of Nancy reveals why making music and, more specifically, making music well, creates occasions of pleasure and contributes to the happiness of the musician. Making music better requires having an appropriate constellation of meanings to associate with the sounds that the musician encounters when playing the musical score. The musician will listen: will encounter the sounds, feel them reverberate with previously established meanings, and be able to make sense of the sounds so as to meet the relevant standards of excellence. Pleasure occurs when the musician meets the standards. Thus, pleasure accompanies music made well and making music well moves the musician in the direction of happiness.

We are not saying that either Deborah or Sophie is happy, given Aristotle's understanding of that term. Indeed, he tells us that "one swallow does not make a summer, nor does one day [make a summer]; and so too one day, or a short time, does not make a man blessed and happy" (1098a, pp. 17–20). Here we take Aristotle to mean that achieving excellence occasionally is not sufficient to render a person happy. We claim only that a necessary condition for the happiness of a musician—someone who wants to make music and who does, or tries to do, things that will achieve the goal of making music—is making music *well*. The musician who makes music well is going in the direction she needs to go if she is going to be happy. In order to get better at making music, the musician must develop an ever more appropriate constellation of meanings, which are then used to make sense of the sounds she encounters. With such a constellation comes the possibility of the musician playing the music even better than before. As the musician continues to improve her playing of the music, she experiences more occasions of pleasure, which in turn contribute to her happiness.[4]

4

SECHS MOMENTS MUSICAUX

Komponiert wahrscheinlich 1823–1828

HEFT I

Opus 94 · D 780

Moderato

1.

Figure 8.1 Franz Schubert's *Moments Musicaux Number One*, p. 4.

Figure 8.1 Continued

Notes

1. All page references are to Aristotle, *Nicomachean Ethics,* in Jonathan Barnes (1984).
2. In following our narrative, the reader should consult both the musical score (see end of chapter) and the transcript excerpts from the lesson presented throughout. Each transcript excerpt is divided into lines that are given numbers. Words that appear in parenthesis describe things that occurred in the lesson; words that appear in brackets are added for clarification of what took place.
3. Quotations are taken from the Mandell translation of Jean-Luc Nancy's text, *À l'écoute,* as it is assumed that most readers will read Nancy's work in the English translation.
4. We wish to thank Gareth Dylan Smith and Marissa Silverman for their comments on an earlier draft of this chapter.

References

Aristotle. (1984). *The complete works of Aristotle: The revised Oxford translation.* J. Barnes, (Ed.). Princeton, NJ: Princeton University Press.

Nancy, J. L. (2002). *À l'écoute.* Paris: Editions Galilee.

Nancy, J. L. (2007). *Listening* (C. Mandell Trans.). New York: Fordham University Press.

Nancy, J. L. (2013). Récit Recitation Recitative. In K. Chopin & A. H. Clark (Eds.), *Speaking of music: Addressing the sonorous* (pp. 242–263). New York: Fordham University.

9 Eudaimonia and Well-Doing

Implications for Music Education

David J. Elliott

Philosophers have explored the nature of eudaimonia—often simplified to human flourishing—for over two millennia and continue to debate and revise concepts of eudaimonia today. In this chapter I discuss a philosophical approach to eudaimonia that integrates relationships between ethical individual and/or collaborative well-doing, well-being, and, to some degree, personality. My goal is to provide a provisional explanation of why and how eudaimonia relates to the agency and chosen actions of "well-doing," where "well" doing means ethically-guided doing/action, or "right" action," that is or can be carried out by amateur musicians.

I will explain more about the meaning of "amateur" in a moment. But for now, and because this book is about eudaimonia and music education, I will simply say that the term amateur is exemplified in nearly all forms of school music making in concert bands, jazz bands, choral and string/orchestra groups, popular music groups, various forms of music technology configurations (and so forth) that music students engage in during their school years, depending on their local, regional, or national contexts (e.g., K-12 in the United States). In addition, the term amateur is exemplified by what occurs in community music groups that adults organize for children and youth, such as the Brooklyn Youth Chorus (New York City) and the Bow-Dacious String Band (Urbana, IL, U.S.), which is for children and youth from 6 to 18. The Bow-Dacious String Band plays traditional dance and fiddle music, folk songs, and blues, pop and rock music.

More about the meaning of "amateur" momentarily.

Of course, musical well-doing also applies to what many professional musicians around the world choose to do beyond their contracted performance duties, like members of the Chicago Symphony Orchestra who make their living by performing, but who also perform for charitable and social justice causes, or give free lessons and chamber music concerts to marginalized youth. But as I noted earlier, professional music making is not my concern in this discussion.

Clarifying Two Basic Terms/Concepts: Ethically-guided Actions and Amateur

Let me begin with actions or "doings" that are *not* ethically-guided; put another way, they are *not* examples of well-doing, but of wrong-doing. Unethical actions or wrong-doing(s) include, for example, human and animal torture and genocide. Notably, and on a very large scale, Syria's brutal dictator Bashar Hafez al-Assad has, for many years, ordered his armed forces to slaughter Syrian civilians who attempt to oppose his regime.

In terms of unethical musical actions, the famous German conductor Herbert von Karajan frequently conducted the operas of Richard Wagner, a virulent anti-Semitic composer, for Adolf Hitler and the Nazi elite. Indeed, Karajan made the deliberate decision to continue conducting and recording—to engage in unethical wrong-doing—in Germany throughout the period of the Third Reich, thereby displaying his public support for Hitler and his murderous dictatorship, and feeding his egotistical needs for musical/public recognition and promotion.

In contrast, the outstanding conductor Erich Kleiber, "unerringly opposing the Nazis, not least because of their anti-Semitic policies," left Germany for Argentina during the Third Reich (Kater, 1997, p. 123). Kleiber could have continued his conducting career in Germany, but acting ethically: Kleiber condemned "the silencing of famous Jewish composers, such as Meyerbeer, Mendelssohn, Mahler, and Offenbach" (Kater, 1997, p. 123). Additionally, Kleiber rejected his contract with La Scala in Milan in 1939, stating:

> I hear that access to the Scala is denied to Jews. Music, like air and sunlight, should be for all. When in these hard times, this consolation is denied to a human being for reasons of race and religion, then I, both as Christian and artist, feel that I can no longer co-operate.
>
> (no author, Musical Notes from Abroad, 1939, p. 306)

More generally, as my co-author Marissa Silverman and I argue in *Music Matters: A Philosophy of Music Education* (2015), ethics is "reflective, practical, and social because we always think and act in languages, experiences, and situations we share with others" (p. 20). And because ethical thinking and doing concerns what and how each of us decides how we ought to live and act in relation to the daily challenges we face in our personal and interpersonal lives, it follows that our ethical well-doing is central to our individual identities (Elliott & Silverman, p. 20). It involves "developing an identity, [which is] enmeshed in larger, collective narratives" (Appiah, 2005, p. 231). Ethics is also at the center of our social roles—doctor, lawyer, teacher, musician, parent—and our sense of belonging, "of being situated within a larger narrative or narratives" (Appiah, 2005, p. 231) and acting rightly *in situ*.

So, ethically-guided doing is centrally related to personal and/or interpersonal projects and related social groups that children and young people engage in and with which they may decide to identify.

Additionally, and notably, there is no consensus on what "amateur" means. Like all terms and concepts in music education and community music, it's an "essentially contested concept": it's an historically, culturally, emotionally, ethically, practically, politically, value-laden, and unstable idea that resists a conclusive definition or formulation (Elliott & Silverman, 2015, p. 9). Thus, the best I can do here is to offer some basic themes that sketch the outline of the concept.

Etymologically, the term amateur derives from the Latin root "amat," meaning "lover" (Regelski, 2007, p. 27). Robert Booth (1999) coins the term "amateuring" to encapsulate the characteristics of an amateur pursuit, which Regelski summarizes as the "active, committed, disciplined (or 'dis-cipled'), enlivening, and loving pursuit of, in our case, music" (p. 27). He argues that amateuring is not mindless, idle dabbling, but to the degree that a participant has the time, means, and energy to pursue it, it can be vigorous, compelling, and demanding. As Booth (1999) says, "the amateur works at it … aspiring to some level of competence or mastery or know-how or expertise" (p. 12). As a result:

> the joys of amateuring deserve celebration of a kind undeserved by many leisure-time rivals. Amateuring is totally different from enjoying a time-killer or mere escape from boredom. It may be in a sense an "insanity," but, like very few other human pursuits, it carries us out of this world, into what I can only call the timeless
>
> (p. 16)

So far, then, the amateur is one who participates in an activity because he or she begins or comes to love it over time, and as her abilities develop in relation to the musical challenges that begin to spiral upward, gradually or quickly. And as/when the amateur's ability level matches the level of the challenges she encounters, she undergoes what Mihaly Csikszentmihalyi (1975) calls the "flow experience," or "optimal experience," that is self-actualizing. Of course, full-time professional musicians are likely to have experienced "flow" early in their musical development and, thus, decided to pursue music making as a profession for this and other reasons. But the difference for the amateur is that (a) the motivation/reason for her participation lies in the intrinsic rewards, including the flow experiences, that derive and accrue from the "doings" of her participation, not the extrinsic rewards of money or fame, which are additional and necessary for the professional musician who depends on his or her income to support herself and, perhaps, a family. In other words, the process is as important as, or more important than, the product of the activity. Put yet another way, amateurs are involved in their musicing because "the process is prize enough" (Eitzen, 1989, p. 102). They are engaged in their doing because they "love it," which is both the necessary and the sufficient condition for involvement. For the amateur, (b) her chosen activity is freely chosen, except in unfortunate cases where students are forced to take music as a school requirement and, therefore, may come to hate it. And (c) following from the concept of well-doings, or ethically-guided actions, it is important that amateur music makers understand that "amateur" is, or should be, understood as an ethical word. Think of the ideals of the Olympic Games – not what they have become more recently—in so far as one's participation in group music making, and respect for one's audience, is a matter of genuine mutual respect, if not of ethical caring (Silverman, 2012, 2013) for one's fellow music makers.

A Happy, Meaningful, Eudaimonic Way of Life

What makes a life "good," happy, and/or meaningful? There are two basic ways of answering and/or conceptualizing this ancient question. One is called the hedonic concept, which emphasizes the lifelong pursuit and satisfaction of pleasurable sensations and urges. The second—according to the eminent moral philosopher Martha Nussbaum (2008) and many other scholars I discuss shortly—challenges the hedonic concept by emphasizing what Aristotle and generations of other philosophers and, in more recent years, positive psychologists call a eudaimonic way of life (Deci & Ryan, 2008). A eudaimonic way of life—a flourishing and meaningful life, and more (as stated later)—occurs when a person continuously "works" to bring about significant, positive, transformative life-goals and life-values for him or herself and others (Elliott, 1995; Elliott & Silverman, 2015). A life well-lived, a eudaimonic way of life, is a life that pursues ongoing self-growth and happiness (in the fullest sense of human flourishing) that follows from critically reflective activities that an ethical person believes and feels are personally and communally valuable. Such a life tends to be richer than a hedonic way of life because pleasures (e.g., wine tasting, enjoying a first cup of coffee in the morning, eating popcorn at a movie, sleeping late on a rainy day) do not usually involve reflective, ethically-guided "right actions" in the sense of actions for one's own and others' self-growth, self-efficacy, health and well-being, the ethical care of others, the capacity to nurture, enjoy, and benefit from social fellowship and, as mentioned previously, the positive transformation of one's own and others' communities. Of course, this doesn't mean that a happy life excludes pleasures altogether. A person can experience both eudaimonic happiness and hedonic pleasures in the process of doing "good work" with and for others.

A further distinction between a hedonic life and a eudaimonic life lies in Thomas Nagel's (1972) interpretation of Aristotle's *Nicomachean Ethics*, "which involves both a rarified intellectualist eudaimonia and a comprehensive eudaimonia, which involves ethical action across life's full range of possible engagements" (Danvers, O'Neil, & Shiota, 2016, p. 324), several of which I'll mention later. Nussbaum and many other philosophers and positive psychologists endorse the comprehensive account as proffered by Nagel and, of course, Aristotle, and by this writer. The comprehensive account argues that eudaimonia can/does arise during and after individual and/or collaborative processes of engaging in activities, actions, and/or projects, or "well-doing(s)," including all humanitarian actions: indeed, a full account of eudaimonia must make every effort to understand the many positive ways people can live meaningful lives (Deci & Ryan, 2008; Nussbaum, 2008; Ryff, 1989).

In other words, a comprehensive account "opens the door to a plurality of good lives—all individuals have their own 'good life' to lead" (Danvers, O'Neil, & Shiota, 2016, p. 324), based on the particular domain(s) that they are passionate about and in which they do well, or want to do well, or, perhaps, at which they excel. Martin Seligman (2002) agrees and argues that the "good/engaged" life is fostered when individuals pursue/engage in things they value and/or are good at—what Seligman calls "signature strengths," such as leadership, story-telling, slam poetry, ethical gaming (e.g., gaming for educational development)—to create a "life in the service of something larger than the self" (p. 263). Examples include a teenager who raises funds to aid survivors of a mass school shooting, which may yield self-satisfaction for herself as she works in the service of something larger than herself, namely the healing of her friends and her community; a physician who knows and feels her life is personally significant because it is devoted to the care of her patients; or where a high school teacher experiences self-satisfaction and intellectual and felt qualities of a eudaimonic way of life because of, and in the processes of, her ethical responsibilities to meet the daily challenges of successfully nurturing her students' growth through her educational skills and understandings and, in so doing, empowering future generations of students to pursue a eudaimonic way of life.

In recent years, some psychologists have suggested that

> engaging in "happiness-relevant activities"… represents one way to facilitate psychological well-being … And having a passion for an activity represents an important type of high involvement in activities that may lead to sustainable positive effects on psychological well-being.
>
> (Vallerand, 2012, p. 1)

Psychological well-being includes "self-acceptance, purpose in life, environmental mastery, positive relationships, autonomy, and personal growth" (Danvers, O'Neil, & Shiota, 2016, p. 326). Other scholars (e.g., Deci & Ryan,

2008) posit a similar view, but add that truly eudaimonic actions must contribute to our own and others' needs for "autonomy, relatedness, and competence" (Danvers, O'Neil, & Shiota, 2016, p. 325).

Eudaimonia, Well-Doing, and Passionate Obsessions

Implicit and explicit in everything I have said thus far is the claim that a eudaimonic way of life depends centrally on actions—on critically reflective, passionate engagements, and ethical pursuits that individuals and/or communities find enjoyable, valuable, meaningful, significant, and communally transformative, as I've reiterated from the outset.

So, now, let us view eudaimonia through the lens of "well-doing" because, as Brian R. Little (2016) says:

> A shift away from the various states of happiness and well-being to the activity that creates such states would be a concession not only to Aristotelian conceptions of human flourishing but also to other philosophical traditions in which action and its consequences are pivotal to understand the human good. From such a perspective, human flourishing comprises the sustainable pursuit of core projects in one's life.
>
> (p. 307)

Closely linked to well-doing are the deep emotions—the passionate obsessions— that people develop for the activities they choose to engage in. A passionate obsession is a deep devotion to and motivation for carrying out the pursuits that individuals choose to do and, of course, which thousands of others often do, too. Passionate obsessions often include collaborations between/among a few individuals and/or large communities of participants in much wider communities (local, regional, national, and international). More precisely, a "passionate obsession" for an activity is defined as "a strong inclination toward a self-defining activity that one loves and finds important, and in which one invests a substantial amount of time and energy" (Elliott & Silverman, 2015, p. 197). Passions for self-fulfilling, intrinsically motivating activities—including the amateur social praxes of gardening, dog training, embroidery, cake making, curling, figure skating, and so forth—are often "contagious": for example, many children "automatically" imitate or model, adopt, and invest emotions in their parents', siblings', or friends' passions for the well-doings mentioned earlier.

Robert J. Vallerand (2012) adds another layer of values and complexity to the concept of well-doing when he discusses self-identity. He argues that when people become positively engaged in something they value and enjoy, and pursue it frequently and enthusiastically, then the activity becomes part of their identity and, often, a source of self-esteem and self-efficacy (p. 3).

For example, children who are introduced to, develop an interest in, and become passionate about playing amateur basketball or songwriting often begin to see, feel, and think of themselves as "real" basketball players or singers, or become passionate fans/followers of their favorite players, teams, musical styles, stamp collectors, and so forth. In sum, a passionate activity is also something that can shape a person's sense-of-self in many important and complex ways. The activity becomes an inherent part of who a person is to herself and to others.

In view of the values discussed earlier and shortly, it seems appropriate to suggest that any reader who finds these values academically "soft," extramusical, or irrelevant to music education and community music may want to consider Clive Beck's (1974) observation: What these values have in common is the fact that ethically-guided people seldom ask, "Why do you want … happiness, health and well-being, enjoyment, self-worth, fellowship, and similar values?" (p. 21).

At this point, it may be useful to differentiate a passionate obsession from an harmonious passion. The only real difference between the two—but still an important distinction—is that sometimes people who love doing something too much, who are truly obsessed by it, can be overcome with an uncontrollable urge to continuously engage in it in a self-destructive, impulsive, or addictive way, which often overwhelms their lives: for example, compulsive internet gamers. In contrast, an harmonious passion is one in which "the activity occupies a significant but not overpowering space in the person's identity and is in harmony with other aspects of the person's life" (Vallerand, 2012). Even more positively, an harmonious passion tends to encourage and motivate regular, intrinsic, and integrative experiences that energize participants to experience positive emotions on a regular basis which, in turn, increases the likelihood of sustainable psychological well-being (Ryan & Deci, 2001).

Meaning and Meaningfulness

Another important dimension of the sustained pursuit of harmonious passions for, and results of, eudaimonic well-doing and well-being is the sense that one's life is meaningful and significant (Halusic & King, 2013; Ryff, 1989; Ryff & Singer, 2008; Steger, 2012). Why are meaningfulness and significance so important? Because everything scholars have said about comprehensive human flourishing includes making an effort to bring about positive transformations in one's own and others' life-goals and life-values, which logically and necessarily means that individuals and allied groups of people do so for and with a sense of purpose and, therefore, with personal meaning-making. So, in addition to what I have said so far, a life well-lived, a eudaimonic life is characterized by meaningful living to the point that a life filled with "ongoing self-growth and happiness would *not* be considered to have attained optimal functioning in the absence of meaningful living" (Ryff & Singer, 2008, p. 20). In other words, people who consciously pursue a eudaimonic life have, or cultivate, a strong inclination to find and make meaning (Frankl, 1963). Vallerand (2012) adds that "meaning is found in the aims we create for ourselves that extend beyond the present moment, across our lives" (p. 15). Many scholars, past and present, concur (see, for example: Aristotle, *Nicomachean Ethics*, Book II; Baumeister & Vohs, 2002; Heine, Proulx, & Vohs, 2006; Halusic & King, 2013; Jarvis, 2007; Longworth, 2016; Wolf, 2010).

I now turn to key philosophical arguments for meaningfulness, with special attention and indebtedness to two contemporary philosophers: Susan Wolf (1982, 2010) and Marissa Silverman (2013). Silverman starts her discussion with three related questions: What is the meaning of life, and/or the nature and role of meaning in life, and/or how a person decides whether his or her life has meaning (p. 23)? And how does meaning relate to eudaimonia? She (2013, p. 20) points out that many philosophers (e.g., Aristotle, Kant, Bentham) have approached these questions from numerous perspectives. She argues that it's more likely that individuals believe their lives are meaningful because of "what they do or have done," which, of course, aligns with this chapter's emphasis on ethical well-doing. Silverman (2013) cites Tove Pettersen (2011), who integrates interrelationships and care ethics to help explain meaningfulness: "where the starting point is human connectedness and interdependency as it is in an ethics of care, the welfare and growth of one individual is seen as intertwined with the flourishing of others" (p. 5). Pettersen goes on to discuss "mature care," a term coined by Carol Gilligan in 1982: "Mature care seems to highlight the relational aspect of the persons involved in the caring relationships of which each of them partakes" (p. 11). Silverman brings these themes together: "And it's within this sense of self-and-other that we begin to grasp the nature of 'meaningfulness'" (Silverman, 2013, p. 24).

On the topic of meaningfulness and happiness, Silverman turns to Bernard Williams (1981), who proffers that meaningfulness involves an attachment to something that permeates our existence and gives us a reason to live: a person often develops or has "a ground project or set of projects which are closely related to his life" (p. 12). This, too, relates to key points I have made earlier about the central role of actions, projects, and well-doing in people's pursuit of a eudaimonic life. Indeed, Williams (2011) writes that an activity has to appeal to a person in relation to something about himself or herself—about "how and what he will be if he is a person with that sort of character ... who engages in specific actions" (p. 36). And a person must be motivated to pursue projects that share certain things in common. In other words, says Silverman (2012), who we are and what we do are bound together existentially, and desire is a key component in developing a life of meaning (p. 25).

Without desire (or an harmonious passion), says Williams, it is difficult to understand the nature and values of the actions one chooses to engage in, and it is difficult to unpack why a person would take up actions or projects that might not be meaningful to him or her.

Silverman adds nuance and depth to her argument by citing Wolf's emphasis on the interrelations among actions, projects, and love: "when acting from projects of love, rather than out of a sense of duty or obedience, we can reach a space of meaningfulness"; meaningfulness "arise[s] from loving people, objects, and/or activities that are *worthy* of love" (pp. 61–62, italics added). "The most obvious examples of what I have in mind," says Wolf, "occur when we act out of love for individuals about whom we deeply and especially care" (p. 4). So here we see how subjectivity, intersubjectivity, care for others, and love are intertwined. But Wolf does not limit love to doing things for others alone. Doing and loving include loving oneself in the process of engaging in actions that are "good for" one's loved ones and community. Moreover, love(s)

> move us to engage in all sorts of activities and interests that we are dedicated to and passionate about," but "the key issue is whether or not an enjoyable activity is likely to provide the foundation for a continuously meaningful life.
>
> (Silverman, p. 26)

In line with positive psychologists (cited earlier and shortly), Wolf (cited by Silverman, p. 28) says this: "[One] has to actively engage with the worthy object (or activity) in order to bring about meaningfulness." Silverman (2013) agrees: "In other words, such activities immerse me in a rich and diverse web of intersubjective relationships that are valuable and therefore meaningful" (p. 33). Wolf continues:

> Essentially the idea is that a person's life can be meaningful only if she cares fairly deeply about some thing or things, only if she is gripped, excited, interested, engaged or … if she loves something [or someone she is doing something for/with, or someone she loves, including herself].
>
> (p. 9)

In sum, says Silverman, meaningfulness includes a number of philosophical and practical virtues: "hard work, discipline, being part of a community of people that shares my interests … In other words, such activities immerse me in a rich and diverse web of intersubjective relationships that are valuable and therefore meaningful" (p. 33).

Related and relevant to the earlier discussion, many positive psychologists (e.g., Debats, 1996; Debats, van der Lubbe, & Wezeman, 1993; Ryff &

Keyes, 1995; Steger, Oshi, & Kesebir, 2011) have generated a significant body of empirical evidence that supports important intersections between contemporary philosophical work on meaningfulness and key aspects of the comprehensive account of eudaimonia. Taken together, this empirical psychological research has "drawn consistent links between meaning in life and both psychological and physical well-being and one's sense of purpose" (Dezutter et al., 2013, p. 336). As emphasized by other scholars (e.g., Keyes, Shmotkin, & Ryff, 2002; Steger, 2006a, 2006b; Thompson, Coker, Krause, & Henry, 2003), meaningfulness in life is positively related to happiness, life satisfaction, self-efficacy, self-acceptance, and self-actualization (Ryff, 1989; Steger, Kashdan, Sullivan, & Lorentz, 2008; Schlegel, Hicks, King, & Arndt, 2011). Researchers have also connected meaning with hopefulness (Feldman & Snyder, 2005) and, relatedly, with efforts to maintain positive views of oneself and develop resilience and agency, "the perceived ability to carry out those plans" (Danvers, O'Neil, & Shiota, 2016, p. 338). Thaïs Helène Dowman (2008) elaborates:

> The importance of a sense of meaning and purpose is a vital component of the human experience. It gives a sense of wellbeing, of peace and contentment, of hope, and facilitates a self-transcendence and connectedness with others who matter to us and something greater than oneself. It helps us to maintain our dignity, honour, [and] esteem … This [Downman's] research concluded that meaning-centered intervention increased spiritual wellbeing and a sense of meaning, reducing hopelessness … A sense of meaning and purpose has also been described in *Man's Search for Meaning* by the psychiatrist Viktor Frankl [1963] who survived in a concentration camp.
>
> (p. 249)

Implications for Music Education

In this concluding section of the chapter, I will expand slightly on the concept of eudaimonia because, to me, the details of this expansion follow logically from the idea that music (and, likely, the other arts) is "good for"—i.e., valuable, as long as ethically-guided well-doing is involved—many things (Elliott & Silverman, 2015, p. 46). First, because of the positive musical-emotional experiences that music making and listening can arouse and express (e.g., Juslin & Sloboda, 2010; Elliott & Silverman, 2015), effective and ethical music education can make major artistic, social, cultural, gendered, ethical, emotional, mental, and political differences in students' and adults' lives. For example, when student performers develop their own interpretations of compositions, and when student composers/improvisers create music—and when they carry out similar forms of well-doing in the contexts of musics of non-Western cultures—then the possibilities for deepening students' musical and personal self-worth, satisfactions, confidence, pride, self-growth, identities, and happiness increase exponentially. In this view, participating in musical praxes is a powerful and exquisite way of growing, thriving, experiencing, and contributing constructively to oneself and one's own sense of meaningfulness and significance in one's own and other's life-worlds.

So, music does not have one value, music has many values. For example, when music education is ethically-guided, when we teach people not only in and about music, but also through music (Elliott, 1995; Elliott & Silverman, 2015), then students and teachers have opportunities to achieve life-affirming and joyful pathways toward achieving a "good life" of well-being, flourishing, and happiness for the benefit of themselves and others. Eudaimonia, then, is the ultimate aim and value of the praxial philosophy of music education that my co-author Marissa Silverman and I (2015) proffer.

Relatedly, when music making is carried out with careful attention to (1) musical expressiveness and many social, cultural, political, and other contextual factors that affect music making and listening, and (2) respect for the people involved in making, listening to, and learning music in specific situations, then music and music education are valuable sources of ethical insight. As educational philosopher Christopher Higgins (2012, pp. 213–230) reminds us, formal and informal sites of music education and community music have the potential to be places where people can develop virtues. Indeed, if we don't step outside our musical involvements long enough to think critically and comprehensively about the natures and values of music (and all the arts), then we will fail to understand what music and music making can teach us about life and living. As Wayne Bowman (2006) says:

> Music, and therefore education in it, is crucial to human flourishing, or eudaimonia, as the ancient Greeks called it. Music teaches us things about our common humanity that are worth knowing, and renders us less vulnerable to forces that subvert or compromise human well-being. Studying and making music changes who we are and what we expect from life.
>
> (p. 39)

Thus, it's not surprising that Aristotle followed Plato in the belief that children should be educated for their productive responsibilities in community life by means of ethical well-doing in guided activities, such as music, that would develop "proper virtues." To Aristotle, this meant providing a balanced curriculum for the whole child. Play, debate, music, physical activities, and the study of science and philosophy were all necessary for the proper formation of the body, mind, and soul. Aristotle emphasized the need to balance theoretical and ethical-practical reasoning, or phronesis, in all well-doing. Like Plato, Aristotle also believed that learning should continue throughout lifelong study, critically reflective actions, interpersonal relationships, and civic engagement, but with emphases that change with age.

In conclusion, developing the many dimensions of knowing and feeling—that educated music teachers and community music facilitators can and do learn to teach—that are required to meet most amateur (in the best sense of "amateur") musical challenges in particular contexts of music—can lead to a eudaimonic way of life. When housed in safe school and community environments where students feel valued, they invariably experience self-growth, self-knowledge, and enjoyment. And this, in turn, leads to a fulfilling sense of eudaimonic personhood.

References

Appiah, K. A. (2005). *The ethics of identity*. Princeton, NJ: Princeton University Press.

Aristotle. *Nicomachean ethics.* (1980). (W. D. Ross, Trans.). Oxford: Oxford University Press.

Baumeister, R. F., & Vohs, K. D. (2002). The pursuit of meaningfulness in life. In C. R. Snyder & S. J. Lopez (Eds.), *Handbook of positive psychology* (pp. 608–618). New York: Oxford University Press.

Beck, C. (1974). *Educational philosophy and theory*. Boston, MA: Little Brown.

Booth, W. (1999). *For the love of it: Amateuring and its rivals*. Chicago, IL: University of Chicago Press.

Bow-Dacious String Band. Retrieved June 9, 2019 from http://c-4a.org/group-music-making/directed-ensembles/bow-dacious-string-band/

Bowman, W. (2006). Educating musically. In R. Colwell & C. Richardson (Eds.), *MENC handbook of research methodologies* (pp. 63–84). New York: Oxford University Press.

Csikszentmihalyi, M. (1975). *Beyond boredom and anxiety: Experiencing flow in work and play*. San Francisco, CA: Jossey-Bass.

Danvers, A., O'Neil, M., & Shiota, M. (2016). The mind of the "Happy Warrior": Eudaimonia, awe, and the search for meaning in life. In J. Vittersø (Ed.), *Handbook of eudaimonic well-being* (pp. 323–235). Basel, Switzerland: Springer.

Debats, D. L. (1996). Meaning in life: Clinical relevance and predictive power. *British Journal of Clinical Psychology, 35*(4), 503–516.

Debats, D. L., van der Lubbe, P. M., & Wezeman, F. (1993). On the psychometric properties of the Life Regard Index (LRI): A measure of meaningful life. *Personality and Individual Differences*, *14*, 337–345.

Deci, E. L., & Ryan, R. M. (2000). The "what" and "why" of goal pursuits: Human needs and the self-determination of behavior. *Psychological Inquiry*, 11, 227–268.

Deci, E. L., & Ryan, R. M. (2008). Hedonia, eudaimonia, and well-being: An introduction. *Journal of Happiness Studies*, *9*(1), 1–11.

Dezutter, J., Casalin, S., Wachholtz, A., Luyckx, K., Hekking, J., & Vandewiele, W. (2013). Meaning in life: An important factor for the psychological well-being of chronically ill patients? *Rehabilitation Psychology, 58*(4), 334–341.

Dowman, T. (2008). Hope and hopelessness: Theory and reality. *Journal of the Royal Society of Medicine*, *101*(8), 428–430.

Eitzen, D. (1989). The sociology of amateur sport: An overview. *International Review for the Sociology of Amateur Sport, 24*(2), 95–105.

Elliott, D. J. (1995). *Music matters: A new philosophy of music education.* New York: Oxford University Press.

Elliott, D. J., & Silverman, M. (2015). *Music matters: A philosophy of music education* (2nd ed.). New York: Oxford University Press.

Feldman, D. B., & Snyder, C. R. (2005). Hope and the meaningful life: Theoretical and empirical associations between goal–directed thinking and life meaning. *Journal of Social and Clinical Psychology, 24*(3), 401–421.

Frankl, V. (1963). *Man's search for meaning: An introduction to logotherapy.* New York: Simon & Schuster.

Halusic, M., & King, L. A. (2013). What makes life meaningful: Positive mood works in a pinch. In K. D. Markman, T. Proulx, & M. J. Lindberg (Eds.), *The psychology of meaning*, 445–464. Washington, DC: American Psychological Association.

Heine, S. J., Proulx, T., & Vohs, K. D. (2006). The meaning-maintenance model: On the coherence of social motivations. *Personality and Social Psychology Review, 10*(2), 88–110.

Higgins, C. (2012). The impossible profession. In W. Bowman & A. L. Frega (Eds.), *Oxford handbook of philosophy in music education* (pp. 213–230). New York: Oxford University Press.

Jarvis, P. (2007). Globalisation, lifelong learning and the learning society: Sociological perspectives. New York: Routledge.

Juslin, P. & Sloboda, J. (2010). *Music and emotion: Theory, research, and applications.* Oxford: Oxford University Press.

Kater, M. (1997). *The twisted muse: Musicians and their music in the Third Reich.* New York: Oxford University Press.

Keyes, C., Shmotkin, D., & Ryff, C.D. (2002). Optimizing well-being: The empirical encounter of two traditions. *Journal of Personality and Social Psychology, 82*(6), 1007–1022.

Little, B. R. (2016). Well-doing: Personal projects and the social psychology flourishing. In J. Vittersø (Ed.), *Handbook of eudaimonic well-being*. Basel, Switzerland: Springer.

Longworth, N. (2016). *The Oxford handbook of lifelong learning*. London: Routledge.

Musical notes from abroad. (1939, April). *Musical Times*, 197.

Nagel, T. (1972). Aristotle on eudaimonia. *Phronesis, 17,* 252–259.

Nussbaum, M. C. (2008). Who is the happy warrior? Philosophy poses questions to psychology. *The Journal of Legal Studies, 37,* 81–113.

Pettersen, T. (2011). Conceptions of care: Altruism, feminism, and mature care. *Hypatia 27*(2), 1527–2001.

Regelski, T. (2007). Amateuring in music and its rivals. *Action, Criticism, and Theory for Music Education 6*(3), http://act.maydaygroup.org/articles/Regelski6_3.pdf

Ryff, C. D. (1989). Happiness is everything, or is it? Explorations on the meaning of psychological well-being. *Journal of Personality and Social Psychology, 57,* 1069–1081.

Ryff, D., & Singer, B. (2008). Know thyself and become what you are: A eudaimonic approach to psychological well-being. *Journal of Happiness Studies, 9,* 13–39.

Ryff, C. D., & Keyes, C. (1995). The structure of psychological well-being revisited. *Journal of Personality & Social Psychology, 69*, 719–727.

Schlegel, R., Hicks, J., King, L., & Arndt, J. (2011). Feeling like you know who you are: Perceived true self-knowledge and meaning in life. *Personality & Social Psychology Bulletin. 37*, 745–756.

Seligman, M. E. P. (2002). *Authentic happiness: Using the new positive psychology to realize your potential for lasting fulfillment*. New York: Free Press.

Silverman, M. (2012). Virtue ethics, care ethics, and the good life or teaching. *Action, Criticism, and Theory for Music Education, 11*(2), 96–122. http://act.maydaygroup.org/articles/Silverman11_2.pdf

Silverman, M. (2013). A conception of "meaningfulness" in/for life and music education. *Action, Criticism, and Theory for Music Education, 12*(2), 20–40. Retrieved from: http://act.maydaygroup.org/articles/Silverman12_2.pdf

Snyder, C., Harris, C., Anderson, J., Holleran, S., Irving, L., Sigmon, S. (1991). The will and the ways: development and validation of an individual-differences. *Journal of Personality and Social Psychology, 60*(4), 570–585.

Steger, M. (2006a). Measure of hope. *Journal of Personality and Social Psychology, 60*(4), 570–585.

Steger, M. (2006b). Imperial globalism, democracy, and the "Political Turn." *Political Theory, 34*(3), 372–382.

Steger, M. (2012). Experiencing meaning in life: Optimal functioning at the nexus of spirituality, psychopathology, and well-being. In P. Wong & P. Fry (Eds.), *The human quest for meaning* (2nd ed.), (pp. 165–184). Mahwah, NJ: Erlbaum.

Steger, M. F, Oishi, S, & Kesebir, S. (2011). Is a life without meaning satisfying? The moderating role of the search for meaning in satisfaction with life judgments. *The Journal of Positive Psychology, 6*(3), 173–180.

Steger, M. F., Shin, J. Y., Shim, Y., & Fitch-Martin, A. (2013). Is meaning in life a flagship indicator of well-being? In A. S. Waterman (Ed.), *The best within us: Positive psychology perspectives on eudaimonia* (pp. 159–182). Washington, DC: American Psychological Association.

Steger, M., Shigehiro, O., & Selin, K. (2011). Is a life without meaning satisfying? The moderating role of the search for meaning in satisfaction with life judgments. *The Journal of Positive Psychology, 6*(3), 173–180.

Steger, M., Kashdan, T., Sullivan, B., & Lorentz, D. (2008). Understanding the search for meaning in life: Personality, cognitive style, and the dynamic between seeking and experiencing meaning. *Journal of Personality, 76*(2), 199–228.

Thompson, N. J., Coker, J., Krause, J. S., & Henry, E. (2003). Purpose in life as a mediator of adjustment after spinal cord injury. *Rehabilitation Psychology, 48*(2), 100–108.

Vallerand, R. (2012). The role of passion in sustainable psychological well-being. *Psychology of Well-Being, 2*(1), 1–21.

Williams, B. (1981). *Moral luck: Philosophical papers, 1973–1980*. Cambridge: Cambridge University Press.

Williams, B. (2011). *Ethics and the limits of philosophy*. New York: Taylor & Francis.

Wolf, S. (1982). Moral saints. *Journal of Philosophy, 79*(8), 419–39.

Wolf, S. (2010). *Meaning in life and why it matters*. Princeton, NJ: Princeton University Press.

Contributors

The Reverend Professor **June Boyce-Tillman** MBE is Professor of Applied Music and convenor of the Centre for the Arts as Wellbeing at the University of Winchester.

David J. Elliott is Professor at New York University, co-author of *Music Matters: A Philosophy of Music Education* (2nd ed.), and author of *Music Matters: A New Philosophy of Music Education.*

Henry A. Giroux is McMaster University Chair for Scholarship in the Public Interest in the Dept. of English and Cultural Studies and a cultural critic.

Sophie Haroutunian-Gordon is Professor Emerita and Director, Master of Science in Education Program 1991–2014, School of Education and Social Policy, Northwestern University.

Megan Jane Laverty is Associate Professor of Philosophy and Education in the Department of Arts and Humanities at Teachers College, Columbia University.

Kathleen Dean Moore, an environmental philosopher, is Distinguished Professor of Philosophy and co-founder and Senior Fellow of the Spring Creek Project for Ideas, Nature, and the Written Word.

David W. Orr is the Paul Sears Distinguished Professor of Environmental Studies and Politics at Oberlin College and a James Marsh Professor at the University of Vermont.

Marissa Silverman is Associate Professor of Music at the John J. Cali School of Music at Montclair State University.

Gareth Dylan Smith is Assistant Professor of Music (Music Education) at Boston University, a founding editor of the *Journal of Popular Music Education*, and a drummer.

Dylan van der Schyff is a performer, educator, and researcher in interdisciplinary musicology. In 2020, he joins the University of Melbourne as senior lecturer in music (jazz/improvisation).

Index

For Product Safety Concerns and Information please contact our EU representative GPSR@taylorandfrancis.com
Taylor & Francis Verlag GmbH, Kaufingerstraße 24, 80331 München, Germany

www.ingramcontent.com/pod-product-compliance
Lightning Source LLC
LaVergne TN
LVHW020636100826
845148LV00012B/2209

* 9 7 8 0 3 6 7 4 9 8 1 3 9 *